When passionate, self-taught home co[ok] future mother-in-law Roshan's chicken was smitten. It was a chicken curry like [never] tasted before, and he knew he had to have the recipe – even if he had to marry Roshan's daughter to get it!

Simon asked Roshan (Rose) to teach him her vast personal collection of recipes, and now in their kitchen a special friendship flourishes. Rose demonstrates her recipes, recalling techniques and quantities from memory, artfully balancing spices and flavours with an instinct honed by half a century of cooking experience. At her side throughout the process, Simon makes exacting notes, weighing, measuring and timing until he has a clear, precise set of instructions. Then, from these instructions, Simon attempts to cook the dishes himself and the results are put to the ultimate test: Simon's wife tastes everything he makes, ensuring that it remains true to the food she has eaten all her life.

This unique book draws on the extensive repertoire of an exceptional home cook, including traditional dishes passed from mother to daughter over centuries, from the family's Gujerati roots in India, through the African influences of Roshan's youth in Uganda and Tanzania, to modern adaptations for life in England today. You will recognise some familiar names – tandoori chicken, biriani, and samosas are all here alongside more unusual, regional specialities – but you'll find their flavours remarkably different from the food available in Indian restaurants. Over 100 straightforward, foolproof recipes ensure impressively authentic results, with the distinctive taste of real Indian home cooking.

"...a beautiful book with a rare hand-made, artisan quality. It is a wonderful collaboration – a faithful record of the instinctive cooking that goes on in a typical Indian household, and an overdue celebration of the unsung skills of the home cook.

Most importantly it is a story of a family's culinary culture, spanning three different continents and many generations. In the old days, recipes would pass orally from one generation to the next but, with changes in lifestyle, that chain is being broken. In this light, the book takes on another dimension and real significance."

Vivek Singh, Executive Chef at The Cinnamon Club

INDIAN FAMILY
COOKBOOK

INDIAN FAMILY
COOKBOOK

Simon Daley *with* Roshan Hirani

Photographs by Salima Hirani

PAVILION

Dedicated to the memories of my grandmother Eileen (my nan), who taught me to love food, and my father-in-law, Madat, who would have been proud.

And to my son Haroun – our future.

Conceived and produced by Giraffe Books
www.giraffebooks.com

Photography by Salima Hirani
Art direction and design by Simon Daley
Food preparation and styling by Roshan Hirani and Simon Daley
Editor: Salima Hirani
US consultant: Constance Novis
Proofreaders: Alyson Silverwood and Siobhán O'Connor
Indexer: Patricia Hymans

Copyright © Pavilion Books 2008
Text and pictures © Giraffe Books 2008

This edition published in 2012
First published as *Cooking with my Indian mother-in-law* in
Great Britain in 2008 by Pavilion Books
An imprint of Anova Books Group Ltd,
10 Southcombe Street,
London W14 0RA

The right of Simon Daley to be identified as the author
of this work has been asserted by him in accordance
with the Copyright, Designs and Patents Act 1988.

All rights reserved. No part of this publication may be reproduced,
stored in a retrieval system, or transmitted in any form or by any
means, electronic, mechanical, photocopying, recording or otherwise,
without the prior written permission of the copyright owner.

10 9 8 7 6 5 4 3 2 1

British Library Cataloguing-in-Publication Data:
A catalogue record for this book is available from the British Library.

ISBN 978-1-86205-984-9

Reproduction by Mission Productions, Hong Kong
Printed and bound by 1010 Printing International Ltd, China

Contents

Introduction

This book is about home cooking. For me, it's the best kind of cooking because it's always done for the purest of reasons: for sustenance and for love. Domestic cooking has deep roots – in all cultures you'll find centuries-old recipes that have been passed down over generations, usually from mother to daughter – but sadly, nowadays good home cooking is a rare and precious thing. Few of us have the time for the kind of comprehensive apprenticeship that can turn skills learned by rote into instincts, which is why, in this book, I've gathered up the recipes of my mother-in-law, Roshan (I call her Rose – a nickname coined by her late husband Madat). In these pages I hope to pass on all I've had the privilege of learning from a woman who has spent more than half a century honing her skills by cooking for her family.

I'll never forget my first visit to Rose's house. She welcomed me into her home in the way she knew best: by offering good food. For a single man who hadn't had a home-cooked meal (well, not one that I hadn't cooked myself) in years, it was such a warm, embracing welcome.

When Salima – the woman who is now my wife – and I arrived at her parents' home in North-West London on that grey, typically un-summery English June day, Madat opened the door and welcomed us with the sunniest of smiles. The scent of onions and spices filled the hallway, wafting and enticing me like a cartoon trail towards the heart of the house. In the spotlessly clean kitchen I met my future mother-in-law (although I didn't know it then), petite and sprightly, with short, dark hair untouched by grey, dressed in an old T-shirt and tracksuit bottoms liberally dusted with flour from making a huge stack of chappatis. The walls of the room were lined with stacks of bulk-bought food: shrink-wrapped multiples of canned tomatoes, industrial-sized cans of cooking oil, and sacks of rice and chappati flour.

A meal was set out on the plastic wipe-clean tablecloth, served up in the dented, well-worn pans it had been cooked in: perfect rice, sitting in a pristine layer undisturbed by stirring; an impressive stack of whole-wheat chappatis, light and fluffy as breeze-blown pillowcases; flat green *guwar* (cluster) beans scented with mustard (a favourite dish of Salima's); and finally, a simple chicken curry with a shimmering tomato broth infused with onions and cinnamon.

We sat down to eat, and the conversation flowed: the beautiful, unpretentious food and warm homeliness of the welcome settled any sense of shyness in me. The moment I tasted that divine chicken curry, the polite respect that I (as a well-brought-up young man) felt for an elder and the mother of my girlfriend erupted into enormous, profound awe. The key to the magic of that moment was the simplicity of it all. The food, served in a most prosaic manner, had an unmistakable poetry of its own.

Like any Brit, I knew and loved Indian food, but the food I tasted on that day was something beyond what I had come to expect. The flavours were cleaner, brighter, more distinct and yet, despite its depth and savour, the food was somehow lighter than I had experienced before.

I think Rose understood my connection with food from that first meeting: aside from deducing that I love to eat (she was flattered by the enormous quantity of chicken I managed to consume), she could tell that I knew something about cooking. We discussed her recipe – she enjoyed making me guess which spices she had used, and praised me when I guessed correctly. From there it was a natural progression to us cooking together and sharing recipes (she now cooks some of my recipes, too), and out of that process this book grew.

A few months after that first meal at Rose's house, Salima showed me a set of photographs she had made of her mum making samosas. She'd stood on the kitchen worktop to look down at Rose's busy hands. I loved the honesty of the pictures – and how they conveyed a genuine understanding of the food. My job as an art director on cookbooks meant that I knew how tricky it is to capture food well on film, and how much work goes into constructing a 'natural' look: but these guileless pictures were engaging and informative. It was unthinkable that anyone but Salima would take the pictures for this book – and in fact no one could have made Rose, a naturally shy person, so comfortable in the gaze of the camera.

We went about the project in a very domestic way: all the pictures for the book were shot in our home, pretty much as we would usually serve them, without tricks or sleight-of-hand. In the writing of each recipe, we've done our best to make even the more elaborate dishes easy to prepare at home with as little need for specialised equipment as possible.

What we all want to highlight more than anything else, in both the words and pictures in this book, is the subtlety and refinement of good Indian home cooking. When I look through my notes about which dishes are favourites, I'm always encouraged to see that it's seldom the elaborate special-occasion foods people love dearly: it's the simple, everyday dishes that they hanker after. Embedded in this fact is a key characteristic of Indian cooking, for me – the magical, almost alchemic transformation of everyday ingredients into something delicious.

In the course of cooking with my Indian mother-in-law I've learned much more than just recipes. In the meandering conversations that have taken place in our kitchen, I've found out about family history and learned all about the culture of the community I've married into. As a new member of Rose's extended family, I've had an opportunity to sample food at many different houses and on special occasions, and I've grown to truly understand the genuine excellence of Rose's cooking. Over time it has become clear to me that she has an instinctive sensitivity to food, one that is always alert and constantly absorbing new ideas. An aspect that emphasises Rose's restless adaptation is her constant work to make her everyday recipes as healthy as possible. Some time ago, she stopped using *ghee* (Indian clarified butter, the traditional cooking fat of North India) and switched to lighter, healthier oils. She weaned her family off white-flour chappatis, and now always makes wholemeal (whole-wheat). She's never been a fan of the sweetness that typifies some Gujarati food, so doesn't sweeten savoury dishes by adding sugar, and recently she's been reducing the levels of salt in her recipes. Seeing this process at work, I've become aware of the subtle evolution of Rose's recipes, and the skill she's applied in adapting them.

But this food has a longer history: many recipes have their roots in the Indian province of Gujarat, from where Rose's family originates. These simple dishes, usually vegetarian, rely on dried beans and lentils, fresh vegetables, yoghurt and wheat, millet or chickpea flours. Recipes of this nature are ancient in origin, but have been progressively adapted over the centuries as they've passed from mother to daughter, shifting with the availability of ingredients, advances in technology and the changing tastes of the passing generations.

Then there are dishes from a time after religious conversion. Rose's distant ancestors converted at some point from Hinduism to a branch of Islam, to become Ismailis – Gujarati Ismailis are more colloquially known as Khojas. The community's immersion in this new culture had a profound effect on its cooking: Muslim dishes were adopted, wonderfully aromatic, with an emphasis on meat – dishes with a noble ancestry tracing back to the Moghuls.

Many Khojas, like Rose's parents, moved on to pastures new in East Africa early last century, taking with them their distinctive cuisine melding the traditions of Hindu and Muslim cooking. On African soil, another influence was assimilated into the mix, resulting in Indian-ised versions of local dishes and Indian recipes modified for African ingredients. Below the English names of the recipes, we've given the name Rose uses to describe the dish – most of the time it's Gujarati, but you'll also see Hindi and a peppering of Swahili, and even English that has crossed over and has no equivalent. Such is the assimilative swell of Khoja culture that there have been times, when we've tried to translate names, that Rose has been surprised to discover that she has no word but the English (and sometimes didn't realise she was using an English word until I pointed it out).

The provenance of these recipes is a complex, multilayered matter. They've passed into my hands via a multitude of hands (such as those of Rose's mother, Rhemat, who taught her how to cook): all have left their mark along the way. For the most part, my involvement has been simply recording. I've tried my best to make accurate records of quantities and important techniques. A careful, even obsessive, eye for detail has served me well: when the time comes for me to cook the recipes I've been taught, I've often found that, having observed every movement and measured every ingredient, the dish I produce is almost identical to Rose's. She has been as pleasantly surprised at this as me: she's never measured, timed or formally recorded any of her cooking, but has been thrilled by the consistency of the results. What thrills me is being able to share these wonderful recipes, in a way that's true to how they're cooked and eaten in many Indian homes, as part of the fascinating ongoing story of mixing cultures in the world today.

Simon
(and Rose)

Basics

One of the joys of learning these recipes from someone who's been making many of them for fifty years is that I've been able to pick up all kinds of hints and tips – wisdom beyond my years. One thing I've discovered is that, where raw ingredients are concerned, Indian cooking is like any cooking: the better the ingredients, the better the end results. For this reason, I've spent some time compiling notes on the best ingredients for the job, how to select and store them, and which ones are the true essentials. Equally important, though, is technique: spending time at Rose's side has shown me that Indian cooking has a method and rhythm of its own, one that's not necessarily known to cooks from other parts of the world. You'll find recipes for some essential spice blends here, and guidance on making a *masala*, the foundation stone of all of the curries in this book. The method of preparing this intensely flavoured, concentrated sauce is crucial to the quality of your finished dish. I urge you to pay careful attention to the notes and pictures on the next few pages: they will stand you in good stead as you set out to cook our recipes.

TO KEEP SPICES FRESH, Rose stores hers away from sunlight in a traditional stainless-steel container known as a *masala daba*. It has separate compartments for spices and two lids to keep it airtight. When the lids are removed the basic palette of spices is handily exposed, ready for use at the stove. Rose has two of these: in one she keeps the most commonly used spices and in the other are whole, sweet spices, which are used less frequently.

The principles of a *masala*

Masala means 'mixture': it can refer to a blend of dry spices, as in *garam masala* or *tandoori masala*; or it can refer to the rich, reduced sauce that is the first stage of so many of the recipes in this book. The *masala* is the key to the final flavour of the curry – in the process of its preparation the aromatics are infused, spices tempered and mellowed, and the sauce amalgamated before the addition of meat, fish or vegetables. The techniques involved in the making of a *masala* are not complex or demanding, but they are incredibly important.

Before I began learning recipes from Rose, instruction on this vital process wasn't something I'd come across in my sizeable collection of Indian cookbooks. Paying careful attention to this stage of the curry-making process made the difference between being able to cook a passable dish and a sublime one.

Making a *masala* is easy, especially if you prepare your ingredients before you cook. Chop onions, prepare the garlic-ginger paste, measure out the spices and set them by the stove. Then, once cooking begins, you can work seamlessly.

Frying onions

In Indian dishes, onions are usually cooked for longer than in Western dishes. Fry your onions over a moderate heat, stirring frequently until they turn a rich golden-brown, or 'pink' as Rose says (see picture opposite, top right). This can take around ten minutes or so, but be patient – the flavour they give to the finished dish is essential and cannot be satisfactorily achieved more quickly. In many of our recipes, once the onions are golden-brown, the garlic, ginger and spices are added (see opposite, bottom left) and cooked briefly, before a little water is poured in and all is cooked down to a slushy, thickened paste. This means that later, when tomatoes are added and the *masala* is simmered to completion, the onions will have disintegrated to thicken the sauce (see opposite, bottom right), while their flavour permeates the entire dish.

Tempering spices

Whether or not onions are used, an essential part of making a *masala* is the tempering of the spices. By this process, the raw and singular flavours of the separate spices are mellowed down to a harmonious balance. A curry can be ruined by the taste of raw or burnt spices, so a little care should be taken over this stage.

Generally, there are three distinct ways in which spices are tempered. Our recipes will always take you through the appropriate tempering stages, but, to introduce them:

Whole, sweet spices such as cinnamon, cloves, cardamom and peppercorns, if used, are normally added to the oil at the beginning of cooking, to infuse the oil as the onions cook gently. Usually, this is done slowly to extract maximum flavour and aroma from the spices.

Whole seeds – cumin, mustard and fenugreek – are tempered in a special preparation known as a *vagar*. The oil is heated to a high temperature

and, in it, the seeds are popped. This usually involves adding a whole dried red Kashmiri chilli to the oil first and, as it blackens, the spice seeds are thrown in. They will splutter and fizz around the pan and, in the process, their flavour is released and mellowed. Curry leaves and/or powdered asafoetida are sometimes added at this point. A *vagar* can form the initial stage in the making of a *masala* (to which tomatoes and vegetables will be added to make a curry). Sometimes, however, a *vagar* is prepared separately, and the spiced oil tipped over a pan of cooked food as a final, aromatic flourish.

Ground spices need to be tempered with care – because they're powdered they can burn easily. In some dishes, they're added to hot oil after popping some seeds and cooked very briefly before liquid is added, to roast them and release their flavour into the oil.

At other times, spices are added after the liquid to guard against burning – when this happens it is particularly important that the *masala* is cooked until the oil pools around the sides of the pan (see below). This ensures the spices are tempered – their raw flavours are cooked away and maximum flavour extracted.

Aromatics

More often than not, garlic and ginger (and sometimes chilli or cumin seeds) are pounded to a paste with coarse salt to add to the *masala*. You could use a blender, although the quantities are small and may not be effectively pulverised. Rose has a great gadget for processing small amounts of garlic and ginger which she uses often but, I rather enjoy the ritual of pounding them using a pestle and mortar.

The timing of when the resulting paste is added can subtly affect the flavour of the finished dish. It can be added to hot oil, to temper its flavours and make them more 'roasted'. At other times it's added to the tomatoes for a stronger, fresher presence. In a few dishes, a little reserved uncooked paste is added in the last few minutes of cooking to give a bright, pungent note to the *masala*.

Tomatoes

A distinctive feature of East African *Khoja* cooking is the liberal use of tomatoes to create the body of the *masala*. In Rose's youth there was an almost year-round abundance of fresh, flavoursome and cheap tomatoes in Uganda. The anaemic hothouse tomatoes that tend to be widely available are comparatively flavourless; canned Italian plum tomatoes make an excellent and less variable substitute. Before you add them, it's a good idea to crush them with their juice as this will help to achieve a smooth *masala*. Once tomatoes are added to the *masala*, it's cooked rapidly to reduce it and thereby intensify its flavour.

When the oil pools

There is a magical moment in the process of making a *masala* when you know it is ready. After a short simmering, the sauce will thicken and the oil that was put in at the start will separate from the body of the *masala*. Tinged with spices, it will pool around the sides of the pan (see picture on page 13, bottom right). When this happens, you can be sure that the *masala* is properly tempered, ready for the addition of the other curry ingredients.

About spices

Indian food is, of course, unimaginable without spices. The complex, multilayered flavours associated with the best Indian food are achieved through careful cooking and the artful combination of usually small amounts of several different spices. In music, single notes are played in combination to form chords – a harmonious melding of the separate elements to form a rich whole. Used correctly, spices can work in the same way, striking their own note yet contributing to an overall, complex effect that is somehow more than the sum of its parts.

Which particular spices are used and how they're cooked will vary slightly depending on the dish and the region from which the dish originates. But throughout India, you'll find the same basic spices used over and over again; at first you'd think that this would mean that all dishes end up tasting the same but, in fact, even a subtle variation in the balance of quantities of each spice, or the method by which the spices are tempered (see pages 12–14) can make a striking difference to the finished flavour.

The beauty of home cooking

You may have eaten in an Indian restaurant and been disappointed to find the flavours in the meat, fish and vegetable dishes to be very similar – it is not unknown for restaurants to have a ready-prepared *masala* which they use as the base for all their dishes. This approach, however, cannot result in anything but unremarkable dishes – one spice balance is not going to suit all foods. This is where home cooking wins over mass production every time: an experienced cook like Rose can tailor the *masala* for each dish specifically to achieve a fine balance between the flavour of the spices and what should be the 'star' of the dish – the main component, be it vegetables, meat or fish.

Spice shopping

Surprisingly, a relatively limited palette of core spices is all you need to cook a huge variety of dishes. Alongside a selection of whole spices, seeds and ground spices (see overleaf), we use two spice blends frequently – *garam masala* and *dhana jiru*. Both can be bought ready-ground but, in the case of *garam masala*, I'd urge you to steer well clear of proprietary blends: they tend to lack character (in aiming to offend no one they also fail to excite). You'll have better results if you take the time to make your own – follow the recipe on page 17. *Dhana jiru*, a classic Indian blend that's used widely, can be surprisingly tricky to get hold of, so we've included a recipe for it too (see overleaf).

We also use two other spice blends in some of our recipes, and these are ready-made blends: hot Madras curry powder and *tandoori masala*. When our recipes use ready-made spice blends, we tend to throw in other pure spices: the blandness of bought spice blends can be successfully alleviated by deft customisation.

Be very fussy about what you buy. Look for Indian blends (and do check the ingredients don't include alien items such as monosodium glutamate, maize starch, and artificial colours or preservatives). Find a brand you like and stick with it. Always buy small quantities and use up your stock quickly so that it remains fresh.

The same advice about buying applies to any ground spices. Buy small amounts and use up quickly. Whole spices keep longer but, unless you're planning banquets, don't bulk buy.

Below are lists of the spices used in the book. Have these in your cupboard, along with some of the basic ingredients (see pages 18–20), and you're all ready to cook. The most commonly used spices are marked with an asterisk*. These are the ones that Rose keeps in her *masala daba*, a specially designed, compartmentalised stainless-steel storage tin (pictured on page 11).

Whole spices

Dried red Kashmiri chillies
Black (or brown) mustard seeds*
Cumin seeds*
Fenugreek seeds*
Coriander seeds (you'll need these for making *dhana jiru*, see below)
Cinnamon sticks or cassia bark (Rose favours cassia – she says it's more flavoursome)
Green cardamoms
Cloves
Black peppercorns
Whole nutmeg
Fennel seeds
White poppy seeds
Saffron strands

Ground spices

Asafoetida
Chilli powder*
Turmeric*

Blends

*Dhana jiru** (see recipe below)
Madras curry powder
Garam masala (see recipe below)
Tandoori masala

Dhana jiru

This simple, roasted blend of coriander (*dhana*) and cumin (*jiru*) is used throughout this book. You may find it in Indian grocers and supermarkets, and online, but you can make it easily yourself – and its freshness is assured if you do. Don't be tempted to mix ready-ground spices to make *dhana jiru* – it just doesn't taste the same (believe me, I've tried it).

To make 560g/1lb 4oz:
350g/12oz coriander seeds
225g/8oz cumin seeds

Preheat your oven to 180°C/350°F/gas mark 4. Scatter the seeds on a baking tray (pan), then put the tray into the hot oven. Roast the spices for 5 minutes (use a timer if you're likely to forget). Remove the tray from the oven and allow the spices to cool completely. Grind to a fine powder in small batches using either a coffee grinder or spice mill.

Garam masala

This mix of roasted sweet spices and chillies is always added at the end of cooking, bringing a sweet, perfumed note to the finished dish. Rose uses *garam masala* mainly in meat dishes: it is too powerful for vegetables, fish and lentils. Recipes vary from region to region and person to person: Rose's version is complex and refined.

To make about 110g/4oz:

50g/2oz cinnamon stick or cassia bark, broken into large pieces

25g/1oz/4 tablespoons cardamoms

1 tablespoon cloves

1 tablespoon black peppercorns

Half a nutmeg

1 teaspoon cumin seeds

2 dried red Kashmiri chillies (optional)

Preheat your oven to 180°C/350°F/gas mark 4. Scatter the cinnamon or cassia pieces, cardamoms, cloves, peppercorns, the half-nutmeg, cumin seeds and chillies (if you're using them – moderate our suggested quantity or omit them altogether to suit your taste) on a baking tray (pan), then put the tray of spices into the oven. Roast for 10 minutes. Remove the tray from the oven and allow the spices to cool completely. Wrap the cinnamon pieces and nutmeg in a clean, dry tea towel and thump with a rolling pin or hammer to smash them into small pieces. Add the broken pieces and any spice 'dust' to the tray of spices and mix them together well. Then grind in small batches in a coffee grinder or spice mill. Sift the resulting powder through a fine-mesh sieve, and put anything that remains in the sieve back through the grinder. Sieve the result and discard anything that remains in the sieve this time around.

Samosa masala

. . . .

This spice mixture adds a distinctive scent and flavour to samosas, but it's only used for this sole purpose and in tiny quantities, so this recipe makes only a small amount. Consider yourselves very lucky indeed to get this recipe – it was something of a secret ingredient of Rose's, and it was with some reluctance and a good deal of

persuasion on my part that she eventually gave me the details. (She has been withholding this information for years!)

To make 25g/1oz of masala:

10g/¹⁄₂oz cinnamon sticks or cassia bark, broken into small pieces

20 cloves (about a teaspoon)

1 teaspoon cumin seeds

3–4 dried red Kashmiri chillies

Preheat your oven to 180°C/350°F/gas mark 4. Scatter the cinnamon or cassia pieces, cloves, cumin seeds and chillies (moderate our suggested quantity to suit your taste) on a baking tray (pan), then put the tray of spices into the hot oven. Roast for 5 minutes, then remove the tray from the oven and allow the spices to cool completely. Wrap the cinnamon pieces in a clean, dry tea towel and thump with a rolling pin or hammer to smash them into small pieces. Add the broken pieces and any spice 'dust' to the tray of spices and mix them together well. Then grind in small batches in either a coffee grinder or spice mill. Sift the resulting powder through a fine-mesh sieve, and put anything that remains in the sieve back through the grinder. Sieve the result and discard anything that remains in the sieve this time around.

Storage

. . . .

All spices should be stored in a cool, dark place, in airtight containers – glass jars are ideal, as long as you don't leave them out where light can get to the spices. Plastic can be tricky to clean and is likely to stain and retain the scent of whatever is stored inside it. A *masala daba*, as shown on page 11, is an excellent way of keeping frequently used spices conveniently to hand.

The Indian storecupboard

An Indian housewife needs to be a mistress of stock control; if you plan to eat Indian meals regularly, you'd do well to follow her example. Rose always has a stock of the basic, recurring ingredients: these she supplements with daily purchases of vegetables, meat, fish and herbs.

In my opinion, the desire for preparedness can go too far: when I can't get to the fuse box in a suddenly darkened house because of the unfeasibly huge sacks of rice and flour stashed under the stairs, I feel the need to draw the line. But there have been many times when I've been only too relieved to get home from work to find that, despite an echoing void of a fridge, there are enough dry goods and cans in the house to make a good meal (for several hundred people!).

Listed here are some fresh and unperishable items, over and above the spices mentioned on pages 16–17, that are useful to keep in stock. I've also given some recommendations for selecting what I feel are the best ingredients for the job.

Oil and butter

Ghee, or clarified butter, is traditional in Indian cooking. It has a distinctive nutty flavour but, in our cholesterol-conscious times, cooking oil is a better everyday alternative, and one that we use throughout this book. In fact, the rich flavour of *ghee* is too heavy for some of Rose's rather refined curries, so a neutral-flavoured oil is best. There are of course some dishes that are special and where a rich buttery flavour is important – in these we have used unsalted butter for a touch of luxury.

There is so much confusing, seemingly conflicting scientific information about the oils we should and shouldn't use in cooking. The key issue seems to be that certain types of oil that are healthy in their raw state become less so when they are subjected to heat. I've frequently specified groundnut (peanut) oil – it's reputedly fairly stable when heated, has a neutral flavour (crucial in most Indian dishes) and produces fine results – but it is only a suggestion. Flavour-wise, sunflower, corn or rapeseed (canola) oils work well too.

Olive oil and mustard oil are used very sparingly in this book, where their specific flavours are desirable – but always ensure that neither of these oils is heated to smoking point.

Salt

Salt is particularly essential in Indian food because its flavour underpins the flavours of chilli and other spices. If you were to try making a hot curry with lots of dried red chilli and leave out salt entirely, the dish would taste unbalanced – leaving you with a pointless, burning-hot sensation without savour. With judiciousness and moderation, salt can make the difference between a dull dish and a delicious one. So, don't forget the salt – but please, don't overdo it. Too much salt is as bad for flavour as too little – and harmful to your health besides.

In most of the savoury recipes in this book salt is pounded with garlic, ginger and chillies. Use sea salt: it has a far superior flavour. I use Maldon salt, and now Rose is an enthusiastic convert. The fragile, flaky crystals are easily crushed in the fingertips for sprinkling, and work well as a gritty abrasive when you're pulverising garlic and ginger using a pestle and mortar. The added benefit of crushing the aromatics with highly absorbent salt is that the essential oils released by crushing are soaked up by the salt. When the resulting paste is added to your cooking, the salt disperses, to carry the flavours throughout the dish.

Garlic and ginger

Our recipes often involve making a paste of just garlic, or both garlic and ginger (sometimes combined with chillies), with coarse salt. Rose, who uses a little of this paste every day, makes up bulk quantities and freezes them.

Look for bulbs of garlic that are firm with well-defined cloves. Big cloves are handy – there's less peeling to do – but if yours are small, increase the quantities slightly to compensate.

Ginger should be smooth, shiny and juicy-looking. Avoid anything dull or shrivelled. To prepare ginger for cooking, peel it as thinly as you can before cutting into slices ready for pounding. Always slice ginger across the grain, to break the fibres and ensure that long threads don't end up in your finished paste.

Chillies

Fresh green chillies are specified often in our recipes. When buying, look for ones that are bright green and crisp, with no dark patches or shrivelling. See my note on page 21 about storing and using chillies and adapting our recipes to suit your preferences in terms of heat, and those of children in the family.

Onions

The onions used throughout the book are predominantly yellow-skinned white onions. Red onions and spring onions (scallions) are used too, often in their raw state. It may seem odd to Western tastes, but Indians have a taste for the crisp, juicy texture and punchy flavour of raw onions: it's not uncommon to see sliced raw onion served up as a simple relish with a curry.

Ready-fried onions

These precooked onions can be bought in supermarkets and Indian stores and are handy for adding instant flavour and body to a curry. Rose and her sister Farida often make a huge batch in Farida's back garden that lasts the extended family's various households several weeks; you can do the same on a smaller scale.

To make your own ready-fried onions, peel, halve and thinly slice a batch of onions. Fill a wok or *karai* to a third of its depth with groundnut (peanut) oil and heat until an onion slice floats and fries immediately. Cook your onions in small batches until golden-brown and crisp, stirring to cook them evenly, then drain thoroughly and blot on kitchen paper. Cool and store in an airtight container lined with kitchen paper – they should keep for several weeks.

Tomatoes

As I've said elsewhere, the quality of fresh tomatoes is pretty unreliable. We've opted for canned Italian plum tomatoes in their juice throughout the book. These have good flavour and colour, and a good meaty texture.

When we specify fresh tomatoes, it's because the recipe calls for a lighter, more delicate flavour than you'd get with canned. Ripe, firm, preferably organic tomatoes will serve well here.

Herbs

Fresh coriander (cilantro) leaves and stems are used in abundance in this book. Buy bunches (rather than cellophane packs from the supermarket). Wash thoroughly as soon as you get home to remove any dirt and grit. Dry well – use a salad spinner if you have one – then bundle up in kitchen paper and slip into a freezer bag. Keep in the salad drawer of your fridge to protect the tender leaves from the cold.

We also use fresh curry leaves and fenugreek greens. They're found in Indian stores and some supermarkets: treat fenugreek as you would coriander (cilantro) – see above; curry leaves should be washed, dried and can be frozen.

Yoghurt

Fresh natural (plain) yoghurt is commonly used in Indian cooking. Don't use either a low-fat or 'set' yoghurt – they tend to curdle when cooked. For best results, use a full-fat yoghurt, preferably one with a good, sharp flavour.

Rice

Basmati rice has a superior flavour, texture and aroma to all other rice (basmati means 'queen of perfume'). Store in an airtight container in a cool place to preserve its fine qualities. Some cooks weigh their rice, but in this book we always use a cup to measure quantities of rice and water (see note on page 72).

Beans and lentils

The key to getting good-quality pulses is to buy them from a reputable source, and one which has a high turnover of stock. Some common lentils and beans can be found in larger supermarkets, but for more unusual ones you'll need to find an Indian grocer, or try online.

Flour

A variety of flours is used in this book, but for the most part they are easily obtainable. Plain (all-purpose), wholemeal (whole-wheat), and strong white bread flours are the major players. If you live near an Indian grocer you may be able to get hold of *atta*, an Indian wheat flour milled specially for bread-making and available in three grades – white, medium and brown.

Millet flour (known as *bajra nu loth*) and chickpea flour (*besan*, gram flour or *channa nu loth*) are sometimes used. You may find them in health food shops as well as Indian shops. Both have a distinctive flavour that deteriorates over time and can turn bitter, so buy small quantities from somewhere with a rapid turnover of stock.

Breads

Although we include recipes for several delicious breads, it's useful to have some in the freezer on standby for quick meals. Pitta bread – white or wholemeal (whole-wheat) – works well with many of the dishes and is easily reheated from frozen. You can buy chappatis and *naan* breads ready-made – although they can't match home-made, they are a useful standby. (Most of our bread recipes freeze well, so why not cook up a batch and stock your freezer with those?)

A note about cooking with chillies

Sensitivity to chilli varies from person to person, as does personal preference – some people enjoy blistering heat, while others are put off by the merest tingle. Spicy heat is part of the authentic balance of Indian food; the flavour chillies impart is just as important to this balance as their heat, but you should be able to taste and enjoy the food you're eating, so adjust our recipes to suit your palate as any Indian housewife would for her family and guests.

Readers wary of the heat imparted by chillies should take a little care when preparing any recipes containing chilli for the first time – the quantities we specify in most cases result in dishes that are medium to medium-hot.

Do remember that chillies and chilli powders vary in strength (the flavour of chillies is affected, like grapes, by the climate and terrain they have grown in, how fresh they are, and their specific variety). In order to reliably customise our recipes for your palate and the strength of the chillies you have bought, we recommend a little methodical experimentation. With fresh chillies (red or green), the first step is to buy a decent quantity – at least a couple of big handfuls – to make sure you will have a chance to get to grips with their potency (don't worry; they freeze well). Look for medium-sized chillies, which tend to be of a medium heat.

When you first cook with a new batch of chillies, err on the side of caution. The seeds and adjoining membranes carry much of the punch (but much of the flavour too, which is why we haven't specified that they be removed in our recipes). Remove them if you generally prefer less heat. If you're concerned by the quantity of chillies specified in the recipe you are preparing in any way, go a step further and reduce it. If the dish turns out too mild (by which I mean the balance of flavours isn't as lively or punchy as you'd like) then at least you'll know you need to increase the quantity of chilli next time, now that you have the measure of the potency of your batch of chillies.

With chilli powder, the procedure is pretty much the same. Buy a decent amount (even brand-name powders will vary in heat, as the chillies they are made from will vary), and be cautious the first time you use it.

Adapting for children

If you love chilli heat, there's no reason to forgo it at family mealtimes. Instead, use one of these methods to get your fix but keep the kids happy:

Sneak them in at the end Make a family-sized portion of your chosen dish, but omit chillies and chilli powder. When cooked, remove enough of the dish for the kids and set aside. To the adults' portion, add fresh chillies to taste and cook for a few minutes to allow their flavour to permeate the dish. Don't add chilli powder at this stage – it will remain untempered and taint the dish with a 'raw' taste.

Sneak them in on the side Make the family meal without chillies, but serve a hot chutney or relish on the side. Try *Sambharo* or *Kachumber* (page 138), or Coriander Chutney (page 132).

Vegetables

Nothing demonstrates the Indian aptitude for assimilation better than the sheer variety of vegetable dishes cooked in Indian homes across the subcontinent and the wider world. All kinds of vegetables – indigenous or introduced from other corners of the globe (such as chillies, tomatoes and potatoes) – are cooked in a multitude of ways, but with an end result that is always unmistakably 'Indian'. When Indians have migrated, as Rose's family did to Africa, they've used whatever produce they found in their new homelands, artfully adapting old recipes to suit new ingredients. As a result, no other cuisine in the world (to my knowledge, at least) can match the breadth of Indian vegetarian cooking. Perhaps this is because the roots of vegetarianism in India are so deep and ancient: Hinduism advocates vegetarianism for health (both bodily and spiritual), and today more than eighty per cent of India's population is vegetarian. This small selection of recipes has Rose's distinctively delicate touch, always ensuring that the intrinsic flavours of the vegetables aren't swamped by unsympathetic spicing or heavy-handed cooking.

UNUSUAL VEGETABLES, alongside common-or-garden potatoes, peas, cauliflower and spinach, appear now and again in this book. You may find them in larger supermarkets, or try an Indian or Asian greengrocer if you're lucky enough to have one nearby. Pictured here (on the worktop and in Rose's hand) are *karela* (also known as bitter gourd or bitter melon) and (in the bag, from left to right) long pods of drumstick (*saragwo*) and bottle gourd (*dudhi*).

Masala-stuffed aubergines
Bharela ringra

Elegantly slender or egg-shaped baby aubergines (eggplants) are used in this curry. A flavoursome *masala* is stuffed inside the vegetables, which are then gently cooked; the result is mellow and richly textured, with the aubergines becoming meltingly tender. Served with Chappatis (page 108) or *Naram Khichri* (page 77), this might just be my favourite thing to eat in the entire book.

400g/14oz slender or egg-shaped baby aubergines (eggplants)

2½ tablespoons groundnut (peanut) oil

½ teaspoon mustard seeds

¼ teaspoon cumin seeds

Pinch of fenugreek seeds

½ teaspoon asafoetida

4 cloves garlic, crushed with ¾ teaspoon salt

4 teaspoons *dhana jiru* (page 16)

½ teaspoon chilli powder

½ teaspoon turmeric

300ml/10fl oz crushed canned plum tomatoes and juice (about three-quarters of a can)

½ tablespoon finely chopped coriander (cilantro) stems

½ tablespoon chopped coriander (cilantro) leaves

For 4, with chappatis or *khichri*

Trim the sepals from the aubergine stems (see picture on page 26, top left), leaving the stems intact – they'll help the aubergines to retain their shape as they cook. If you're using the slender baby aubergines, slice each one in half lengthwise from tip almost – but not quite – to stem (see page 26, top right). If you're using egg-shaped aubergines, cut a cross into the bottom of each one, again slicing almost to the stem, but not quite. Whichever shape you use, put them into a bowl of water as you cut them (this will reduce their bitterness). Lay a small plate on top of the aubergines to fully submerge them.

Put 2 tablespoons of the oil in a pan and place over moderate heat. Add the mustard, cumin and fenugreek seeds. When they're aromatic, but before they pop, add the asafoetida and cook for a few seconds before adding the garlic paste and 1 tablespoon of water. Cook for a minute or so, then add the *dhana jiru*, chilli powder and turmeric. Cook for a few seconds only, stirring constantly, then add the tomatoes and coriander stems. Bring up to simmering point, then cook for roughly 10–15 minutes until the oil pools around the sides of the pan. Remove from the heat and allow the *masala* to cool a little.

Drain and dry the aubergines. Gently open each one with your fingers and, using a teaspoon, smear a generous amount of *masala* as far inside as you can (see page 26, bottom right). Place the stuffed aubergines in a wide pan (one with a lid), in a single layer if possible. Spoon any remaining *masala* in between the aubergines, then trickle over the remaining ½ tablespoon of oil. Cover the pan with foil, then the lid, and set over a low heat. Cook for 15–20 minutes until the aubergines are tender (be careful not to overcook or they will collapse). Serve hot, sprinkled with the chopped coriander leaves.

»*see pictures on the following pages*

Aubergine and potato curry
Ringra bateta nu saak

I'm extremely partial to this classic Gujarati vegetarian curry, especially when served with *Chuthi Khichri* (page 74). When it's made with egg-shaped baby aubergines (eggplants) it's very pretty but, if you can't get hold of them, use regular aubergines cut into large pieces. It will still taste wonderful, the silky aubergine and tender potato becoming deliciously infused with the rich tomato *masala*.

....

450g/1lb aubergines (eggplants) – about 14 baby aubergines or 2 medium-sized ones

4 medium potatoes, peeled

4 tablespoons groundnut (peanut) oil

$\frac{1}{2}$ teaspoon mustard seeds

$\frac{1}{2}$ teaspoon cumin seeds

Pinch of fenugreek seeds

$\frac{1}{2}$ teaspoon asafoetida

4 cloves garlic, crushed with $1\frac{1}{2}$ teaspoons salt

4 teaspoons *dhana jiru* (page 16)

$\frac{1}{4}$ teaspoon chilli powder

$\frac{1}{2}$ teaspoon turmeric

400g/14oz can plum tomatoes and juice, crushed

1 tablespoon finely chopped coriander (cilantro) stems

1 tablespoon roughly chopped coriander (cilantro) leaves

Serves 4 with chappatis or *khichri*

....

If you're using baby aubergines, trim the sepals (see picture on page 26, top left), leaving the stems intact – they'll stop the aubergines falling apart as they cook. Cut a cross into the bottom of each aubergine, cutting almost – but not quite – up to the stem. If you have medium aubergines, cut them into 4cm/1$\frac{1}{2}$in chunks. Whichever size you use, drop them into a bowl of water as soon as they're cut – this will help reduce their bitterness. Once you've finished, lay a small plate on top of the aubergines to submerge any that are floating.

Peel the potatoes and cut into pieces: if you're using baby aubergines, the chunks should be about the same size as the aubergines; with medium aubergines, cut the potato chunks to about half the size of the aubergine chunks.

Heat the oil in a large pan over low heat and add the mustard, cumin and fenugreek seeds. When they begin to sizzle, add the asafoetida. Cook for a few seconds and add the garlic paste, *dhana jiru*, chilli powder and turmeric. Cook gently for a minute, stirring constantly, then add the tomatoes and coriander stems.

Increase the heat to high and cook until the oil pools around the sides of the pan. Drain the aubergines and add them to the pan with the potatoes. Stir carefully to coat with *masala*, reduce the heat to medium and cover the pan. Cook, stirring from time to time, until the vegetables are tender. If they stick, add a couple of tablespoons of water to loosen the mixture. If you're going to eat this curry with breads, keep the mixture fairly thick. If you plan to eat it with *khichri*, add 250ml/8fl oz/1 cup of water towards the end of cooking for a thinner consistency. Serve sprinkled with chopped coriander leaves.

Potato and onion curry
Dungri bateta nu saak

For a change, onions play a starring role in this inexpensive, tasty curry. This is great when you've very little in the house to cook with, or if you're strapped for cash, but please don't think that means this dish is just dull bulk. Careful cooking and a delicate balance of spices make this quite delicious: my wife adores it.

This curry makes a nice light lunch with Chappatis (page 108) or Naan (page 114), a little yoghurt and a leafy salad.

6 medium onions

3 tablespoons groundnut (peanut) oil

2 potatoes, peeled and cut into 5cm/2in cubes

1 fat clove garlic, crushed with 1 teaspoon salt

$3\frac{1}{2}$ teaspoons *dhana jiru* (page 16)

$\frac{1}{2}$ teaspoon chilli powder

$\frac{1}{2}$ teaspoon turmeric

1 tablespoon chopped coriander (cilantro) leaves

For 2 hungry people with chappatis or *naan*

Cut each onion in half from stem to tip. Lay each half down flat on your chopping board and cut each half in half again. Trim the roots and peel off the papery outer skins.

Heat the oil in a wide pan and add the potatoes and onions. Toss the vegetables in the oil, then cover and cook over medium heat for about 5 minutes, stirring from time to time, until the onions have wilted.

Add the garlic paste to the pan with the *dhana jiru*, chilli powder and turmeric. Stir well and cook gently for a couple of minutes to temper the spices. Then add 2 tablespoons of water, reduce the heat and cover the pan. Cook, stirring occasionally, until the potatoes are tender when pierced with a skewer.

In the last few minutes of cooking, remove the lid to allow excess moisture to evaporate – you can increase the heat a little if necessary (this should be a dry curry). Serve immediately, sprinkled with the chopped coriander leaves.

Cauliflower, potato and pea curry
Ful ghobi bateta ne mattar nu saak

The mixture of colours and textures in this curry is lovely – and the combination of mustardy cauliflower, sweet peas and earthy potatoes in a delicate, fresh-tasting *masala* strikes just the right note. However, you can adapt the recipe successfully to suit what is available: use cabbage instead of the cauliflower or corn instead of the peas, for example. If you are short of one of the vegetables, don't worry: leave it out and increase the quantity of those you do have, and you'll still have a tasty vegetarian curry. Serve with Mustard-pickled Chillies (page 125) and Chappatis (page 108) for a healthy light lunch.

3 tablespoons groundnut (peanut) oil

½ teaspoon mustard seeds

½ teaspoon cumin seeds

Pinch of fenugreek seeds

½ teaspoon asafoetida

1 medium cauliflower, broken into 2.5cm/1in florets (retain the pale, tiny innermost leaves and finely shred them)

2 potatoes, peeled and cut into 2.5cm/1in pieces

2 teaspoons *dhana jiru* (page 16)

½ teaspoon chilli powder

½ teaspoon turmeric

50g/2oz/½ cup frozen peas

3 cloves garlic, crushed with 1 teaspoon salt

135ml/5fl oz crushed canned plum tomatoes and juice (about a third of a can)

½ tablespoon chopped coriander (cilantro) leaves

Serves 4 with chappatis

Heat the oil in a wide pan (one that has a lid), getting it quite hot before adding the mustard, cumin and fenugreek seeds. When they begin to pop, add the asafoetida and cook for a few seconds before adding the cauliflower (and the shredded leaves) and potatoes. Turn the vegetables in the spiced oil, then reduce the heat to low. Add the *dhana jiru*, chilli powder and turmeric and stir the vegetables carefully to coat with the ground spices.

Add 6 tablespoons of water to the pan, then cover and cook gently for about 20 minutes until the vegetables are almost cooked: test them with a skewer or the point of a knife – some firmness should remain at the centre of the potatoes. At this stage, add the peas, garlic paste and the tomatoes. Stir gently and cook for 5–6 minutes longer without the lid, until the vegetables are tender. Sprinkle with the chopped coriander leaves and serve immediately.

ROSE SAYS, to preserve the goodness (particularly the calcium) of the cauliflower, it is best washed *before* you cut it. A good way to do this is to strip off the leaves and submerge the upturned head in a bowl of cold water. Let it stand for a few moments, then drain and break into florets.

Pea curry
Mattar nu saak

Peas – fresh or frozen – make a delightful, delicately flavoured curry with a slight sweetness. Eaten with Chappatis (page 108) or *Naan* (page 114), this dish makes a lovely simple meal, but it also works particularly well as part of a larger meal – the unusual flavour complements many other curries. Fenugreek seeds and asafoetida are not included in the spices as they tend to be in many vegetarian recipes – this, and the fact that the curry is cooked quickly, ensures the freshness of the peas shines through.

....

2 tablespoons groundnut (peanut) oil

1 dried red Kashmiri chilli, broken in half

1/2 teaspoon mustard seeds

1/2 teaspoon cumin seeds

4 tablespoons crushed canned plum tomatoes and juice

1 1/2 teaspoons *dhana jiru* (page 16)

1/4 teaspoon turmeric

1/2 tablespoon finely chopped coriander (cilantro) stems

2 large cloves garlic, crushed with 1/2 teaspoon salt

225g/8oz/2 cups frozen or fresh peas

1/2 tablespoon finely chopped coriander (cilantro) leaves

Serves 2 with chappatis or *naan*, or more as part of a larger meal

....

Put the oil in a smallish pan over medium heat and add the dried red chilli. Let it infuse in the oil and watch as it slowly changes colour (but don't get your eyes too near the pan – the fumes from the chilli can make them smart). Just as the chilli turns black, add the mustard and cumin seeds. They will splutter, so have a lid ready to cover the pan.

After a few moments, add the tomatoes, *dhana jiru*, turmeric, coriander stems and the garlic paste. Stir well and simmer the mixture rapidly until the oil pools around the sides of the pan.

Add the peas and stir well to coat with the *masala*. Cook with the lid on, over gentle heat, until the peas are just tender. (With frozen peas this will take about 5 minutes; with fresh, maybe 10 minutes.) Scatter with the chopped coriander leaves and serve.

Green beans curry
Posho nu saak

Use any green beans for this curry – flat runner beans (cut diagonally into 5mm/¼in slices), Kenya or French beans. Yard-long beans, found in some supermarkets and Asian stores, are particularly tasty if you are lucky enough to find some. Whichever variety you happen to use, the secret to success is in the chopping – keep the pieces small and evenly sized so they'll cook quickly, preserving their flavour. Serve with Chappatis (page 108), Lemon Salt Pickle (page 126) and some yoghurt.

2 tablespoons groundnut (peanut) oil

½ dried red Kashmiri chilli

¼ teaspoon mustard seeds

¼ teaspoon cumin seeds

Pinch of fenugreek seeds

¼ teaspoon asafoetida

350g/12oz green beans, washed, trimmed and cut into 1cm/½in lengths

1 heaped teaspoon *dhana jiru* (page 16)

¼ teaspoon chilli powder

¼ teaspoon turmeric

3 cloves garlic, crushed with ½ teaspoon salt

2 tablespoons crushed canned plum tomatoes and juice

Serves 2 with chappatis, or more as part of a larger meal

Warm the oil in a medium-sized pan. Add the chilli and, as its red colour begins to bleed, add the mustard, cumin and fenugreek seeds. Turn up the heat and, when the seeds begin to pop, add the asafoetida and let it cook for just a few seconds before tipping in the beans. Stir well to coat the beans with the spice-infused oil, then reduce the heat to low.

Add the *dhana jiru*, chilli powder and turmeric. Stir to coat the beans thoroughly, then add 2 tablespoons of water. Put the lid on the pan and cook gently until the beans are just beginning to soften. Add the garlic paste and the tomatoes and cook for a further 2 minutes, stirring constantly. Serve immediately.

Pumpkin and spinach curry
Patkaru bhaji nu saak

Pumpkin is an interesting variation on the more usual potato, although you could happily substitute the pumpkin for potatoes if you wanted to (see my notes below). Use any winter squash you can find – I recommend butternut, kabocha and onion squashes, as they all have a richer, sweeter flavour and denser flesh than regular pumpkin. And look for small ones – they tend to have a more intense flavour.

This makes a nice side dish as part of a larger meal, or serve with chappatis, yoghurt and crunchy red onion slices for a light, tasty lunch.

1 small pumpkin or squash, or half a large one (about 600g/1lb 5oz)

3 bunches of spinach or 2 x 180g/6oz packs fresh leaf spinach, washed thoroughly to remove grit, coarse stems discarded

3 tablespoons groundnut (peanut) oil

$^{1}/_{2}$ teaspoon mustard seeds

Large pinch of fenugreek seeds

2 fat cloves garlic, finely chopped

2 green chillies, sliced

1 teaspoon *dhana jiru* (page 16)

$^{1}/_{2}$ teaspoon turmeric

3 medium-sized tomatoes, skinned and chopped

Serves 2 with chappatis or more as part of a larger meal

Peel the pumpkin and cut into 2cm/$^{3}/_{4}$in cubes. Cut the spinach into 3cm-/1$^{1}/_{4}$in-wide ribbons.

Heat the oil in a wide pan and add the mustard and fenugreek seeds. As the seeds begin to sizzle, add the garlic and the chillies. Cook for 1 minute, then add the pumpkin cubes, the *dhana jiru* and turmeric and stir well.

Trickle 125ml/4fl oz/$^{1}/_{2}$ cup of water down the side of the pan, then cover and cook on a low heat for 10 minutes. Add the tomatoes, stirring carefully, then cover the pan again and cook gently until the pumpkin is tender.

Add the spinach and stir gently to combine. Turn the heat to medium, cover again and cook until the spinach is wilted and bright green. Remove the lid and turn up the heat to reduce excess moisture – a little liquid should remain to lubricate the curry. Serve immediately.

Variations

For spinach and potato curry, follow the method above, replacing the pumpkin with the same weight of potatoes. To make a simple spinach curry, omit the pumpkin, double the quantity of spinach and increase the tomatoes to 4.

Egg and onion curry
Mayai dungri nu saak

A slightly strange-sounding concoction, but really good! Soft, caramelised onions with creamy scrambled eggs make a tasty, inexpensive meal with breads. The sweetness of the onions makes this a good recipe to serve to kids – you can reduce the chilli powder or leave it out altogether if you think they won't like the heat.

2½ tablespoons groundnut (peanut) oil

6 small onions or 4 large ones, halved, peeled and sliced into thin half-moons from root to tip

½ teaspoon salt

2½ teaspoons *dhana jiru* (page 16)

½ teaspoon chilli powder

¼ teaspoon turmeric

1 tablespoon crushed canned plum tomatoes and juice

3 eggs, beaten

1 tablespoon chopped coriander (cilantro) leaves

Enough for 2 greedy people, with chappatis

Put the oil in a wide pan, place over medium heat and add the onions. Fry for a couple of minutes, then add the salt, *dhana jiru*, chilli powder and turmeric. Mix well, then cover with a lid and cook until the onions have wilted.

Remove the lid and cook gently to evaporate any remaining water. This should take about 5 minutes. The onions should be soft and golden, but not browned.

Add the crushed tomatoes and cook for a minute or so, then stir in the beaten eggs. Stir constantly while they cook, as you would for scrambled eggs, until the eggs are set but still soft. Remove the pan from the heat, garnish with the chopped coriander and serve immediately with chappatis.

Bitter gourd with onions
Karela nu saak

Karela, known as bitter gourd or sometimes bitter melon, is a strange-looking green vegetable, shaped like a cucumber but covered in ridges and bumps so that its skin resembles that of a crocodile (see picture on page 23). As its English names suggest, it has a strong, bitter flavour which you'll either love or hate.

Before she was married, Rose cooked this dish often for her father (accompanied by Millet Flatbread – page 117), as *karela* was prescribed for his diabetes. Although it was never popular with her husband's family, Rose continued to cook it for herself because she loved it so much. If you like unusual, strident flavours, give this curry a try – you can often find *karela* in larger supermarkets. They need to be degorged with salt to extract some of their bitterness, unless you can find the smoother, evenly ridged variety that has a fleshier interior and milder flavour. These are the ones that Rose recommends, and they don't need to be degorged.

2 large *karela* (bitter gourd or bitter melon)
Salt for degorging
3 tablespoons groundnut (peanut) oil
2 medium onions, halved and sliced
5 cloves garlic, crushed with 1 teaspoon salt
2 teaspoons *dhana jiru* (page 16)
¼ teaspoon chilli powder
½ teaspoon turmeric
200ml/7fl oz crushed canned plum tomatoes and juice (about half a can)
1 teaspoon brown sugar or jaggery (or to taste)
1 tablespoon chopped coriander (cilantro) leaves

Enough for 2 with millet flatbread or chappatis, or more as part of a larger meal

Slice the *karela* in half lengthwise and scoop out the seeds. Cut into 1cm-/½in-thick crescents. If you have the smoothly ridged variety, skip the next step altogether. If you have the bumpy-skinned variety, put a layer of slices in a colander and sprinkle liberally with salt. Put another layer on top and sprinkle again with salt. Continue layering and salting until all the *karela* slices are in the colander. Stand the colander in a bowl to catch the expressed juices, cover with a clean tea towel and set aside for half an hour. Then discard any juices that have accumulated in the bowl and rinse the *karela* slices in several changes of water. Drain thoroughly and gently squeeze excess water from the *karela*.

Heat the oil in a wide pan and add the onions. Cook gently for 5 minutes or so, until they soften and begin to turn translucent. Add the *karela* and stir gently to mix with the onions. Put on a lid and cook for 10 minutes or so, until the *karela* is almost tender.

Then add the *dhana jiru*, chilli powder, turmeric and garlic paste. Stir gently and cook for 2–3 minutes before adding the tomatoes. At this stage you should lift out a piece of *karela* and taste it to check if you need to add more salt and some sugar or jaggery (you can omit this, but it does balance the bitterness of the *karela* nicely). Cook without the lid now for a few minutes until the *masala* is quite dry. Sprinkle with the coriander leaves and serve.

Okra curry
Bhinda nu saak

Okra makes a surprisingly flavoursome, satisfyingly textured curry when cooked in this way. Rose's trick is to keep the cut vegetable well away from any water, which it will absorb like a sponge, ruining its silky texture and turning it slimy. When buying okra, look for bright, crisp pods with no dark or soft patches.

350g/12oz okra

3 tablespoons groundnut (peanut) oil

½ teaspoon mustard seeds

½ teaspoon cumin seeds

Large pinch of fenugreek seeds

½ teaspoon asafoetida

1 teaspoon *dhana jiru* (page 16)

½ teaspoon chilli powder

½ teaspoon turmeric

3 cloves garlic, crushed with ½ teaspoon salt

Serves 2 with chappatis, or more as part of a larger meal

Wash the okra pods well while they're whole, then drain and dry them thoroughly with kitchen paper. Top and tail the pods, then cut across into rounds about 1cm/½in thick.

Heat the oil gently in a wide pan (one that has a lid). Add the mustard, cumin and fenugreek seeds. After 20 seconds or so, add the asafoetida and increase the heat slightly. When the seeds start to pop, add the okra pieces and toss them in the spiced oil until thoroughly coated.

Reduce the heat to low and add the *dhana jiru*, chilli powder and turmeric, and stir gently. Cover with a lid and cook gently, stirring from time to time, taking care not to break up the pieces. The juices from the okra will run out – keep cooking until they evaporate and the okra is quite soft. The curry should be quite dry. Add the garlic paste and stir well. Cook for a couple of minutes, then serve.

Masala-stuffed okra

Another delicious way to cook okra: follow the recipe for Masala-stuffed Aubergines on page 24, replacing the aubergines (eggplants) with the same weight of okra. (Wash and dry the okra as described above, then cut a slit in each pod from stem to tip before stuffing with *masala*.) Following the instructions on page 24, cook until the okra is tender and has lost its stickiness.

Drumstick with yoghurt
Saragwo nu saak

In this dish, the delicate, asparagus-like flavour of drumstick (see the picture on page 23) is accentuated in a mild, fragrant yoghurt sauce. Rose came by this wonderful recipe by lucky chance: her mother's recipe for drumstick with *dal* was not popular with her husband, so she was looking for other ways to cook the vegetable. One day, at the greengrocer's she saw a man carefully selecting stems of drumstick for his basket – Rose asked him how he was choosing them. He told her to pick fresh, green, crisp stems, neither too thick nor too thin. When Rose asked how he was going to cook them, the friendly man gave her a recipe: Rose went home with a bag of drumstick and tried to emulate what he had described. The resulting dish was a success and soon became a regular request.

2lb/900g drumstick (about 10 stems)

1 green chilli

4 cloves garlic

2 teaspoons salt

2 tablespoons groundnut (peanut) oil

2cm/³⁄₄in piece of dried red Kashmiri chilli

¹⁄₂ teaspoon mustard seeds

¹⁄₂ teaspoon cumin seeds

Pinch of fenugreek seeds

¹⁄₂ teaspoon asafoetida

2 teaspoons *dhana jiru* (page 16)

¹⁄₂ teaspoon chilli powder

¹⁄₂ teaspoon turmeric

250ml/8fl oz/1 cup yoghurt

1¹⁄₂ tablespoons *besan* (gram or chickpea flour)

1 tablespoon chopped coriander (cilantro) leaves

Serves 4 with rice or *Chuthi Khichri* (page 74)

Trim the tips off the drumstick, and cut into 6cm/2¹⁄₂in lengths, pulling away the fibrous outer skin as you cut. Crush the green chilli, garlic and 1 teaspoon of the salt to a paste.

Put the oil in a wide pan over medium heat. Add the red chilli and the mustard, cumin and fenugreek seeds. When they pop, add the asafoetida and reduce the heat to low. Add the drumstick, *dhana jiru*, chilli powder and turmeric and turn to coat in the oil. Set aside 2 teaspoons of the garlic-chilli paste, then add the rest to the pan. Cook for 30 seconds, then add 125ml/4fl oz/¹⁄₂ cup of water and the remaining teaspoon of salt and simmer gently without a lid, for about 10 minutes, until the drumstick is almost completely tender.

Whizz the yoghurt, *besan*, reserved garlic-chilli paste and 500ml/18fl oz/2 cups of water in a blender and, when the drumstick is almost cooked, add it to the pan. Stir constantly and bring to the boil. Add half of the chopped coriander, reduce the heat and simmer for 10 minutes more, until thickened and creamy. Serve sprinkled with the remaining coriander.

TO EAT DRUMSTICK, first break open the pieces of stem along their length with your fingers to reveal the flesh inside. Then use your teeth to scrape the flesh from the tough skin along the length of the stem into your mouth. Discard the fibrous remains discreetly on the side of your plate as you go.

Fish

Every one of the small handful of recipes in this chapter is a firm family favourite. Fish is important in our house; my wife doesn't eat meat, but she does eat fish, so these are dishes we all enjoy together. Surprisingly, amongst East African Ismailis – dedicated carnivores as a whole – fish is seen as a real treat. This is reflected in the fact that many of the dishes here are intended for special occasions. At such times, whole fish (traditionally tilapia, found in abundance in the waters of Lake Victoria) are devoured with great relish, from nose to tail, every bone sucked clean of juicy flesh. When the extended family is together, there's always a scrum for the fish heads, the head being considered the choicest part. But if the heads offend you, simply discard them – no dish will suffer for their absence. Although a few recipes call for fillets, most use whole fish or pieces of whole fish on the bone. Though more fiddly to eat, fish cooked on the bone will have a superior flavour and texture: I think most Indians would agree that this far outweighs any inconvenience.

WHEN BUYING WHOLE FISH for these recipes, opt for convenience and ask your fishmonger to scale and gut the fish for you. When whole fish are called for in our recipes, you can use any thick, white-fleshed, medium-sized fish: tilapia, snapper (pictured), bream (porgy) and sea bass all work beautifully, but go with what looks good on the fishmonger's slab on the day.

Spiced fried fish
Tareli machi

Simple, quick – and a fantastic way to liven up white fish fillets. The dense texture of meaty halibut steaks or fillets works particularly well here. The trick with this recipe is to have your frying pan (skillet) and oil quite hot to start with, to add your fish skin-side down and to resist turning it too soon. Follow these pointers and you'll end up with a deliciously crispy skin and moist, spice-infused fish beneath.

The perfect accompaniments to this would be Basic *Dal* (page 92) as shown in the picture here, or Split Chickpeas and Bottle Gourd (page 94) and plain basmati rice.

350g/12oz thick white fish fillets or steaks, skin scaled and left on

2 teaspoons lemon juice

2 cloves garlic, crushed with 1 teaspoon salt

2½ teaspoons *dhana jiru* (page 16)

½ teaspoon chilli powder

½ teaspoon turmeric

2 tablespoons tomato purée (paste)

2 tablespoons groundnut (peanut) oil, plus extra for frying

Lemon wedges to serve

For 4 as part of a larger meal

Wash the fish and dry it thoroughly, then cut into manageable-sized portions: you want them to be of a size that you can turn over quickly and neatly – the width of your spatula or fish slice would be a good guide. Combine the lemon juice, garlic paste, spices, tomato purée and 1 tablespoon of the oil and smear all over the fish. Place in a non-reactive dish, cover with clingfilm (plastic wrap) and set aside for 20 minutes.

Heat a large, preferably non-stick, frying pan (skillet). When it is hot, use the remaining oil to cover the base of the pan in a thin film. Add the fish, placing it skin-side down. Leave it to cook, without turning, until the underside is crisp – about 2 minutes if the pan is nice and hot. Then turn the fish and immediately reduce the heat to medium-low. Cook until the fish is done – timing will depend on the thickness of the fillets. The fish should just turn opaque all the way through. Remove to a warm plate lined with kitchen paper. Serve hot, with lemon wedges.

Fish curry
Machi nu saak

For this recipe, choose fish in thick fillets with large flakes of creamy flesh. The rich, spicy sauce complements the delicate, subtle flavour of white fish surprisingly well. The fish is just popped into the simmering *masala* for the final few minutes of cooking; this preserves the flavour and texture of the fish beautifully.

Cod would be delicious, but is in such short supply that we should avoid using it; instead try fillets of tilapia, monkfish or red snapper, depending on what suits your palate and pocket.

In our house we usually serve this dish with *Naram Khichri* (page 77), with some yoghurt and spring onions (scallions) on the side. The first time I ate this curry it was with these accompaniments – I liked the combination so much that I have insisted on it ever since.

200g/7oz white fish

3 cloves garlic

1cm/$\frac{1}{2}$in ginger

$\frac{1}{2}$ teaspoon salt

1$\frac{1}{2}$ tablespoons groundnut (peanut) oil

$\frac{3}{4}$ teaspoon Madras curry powder

1$\frac{1}{4}$ teaspoons *dhana jiru* (page 16)

$\frac{1}{2}$ teaspoon chilli powder

$\frac{1}{4}$ teaspoon turmeric

1–2 green chillies, quartered lengthwise

1 tablespoon chopped coriander (cilantro)

3 tablespoons ready-fried onions (or 4 medium onions prepared as described on page 19)

400g/14oz can plum tomatoes and juice, finely crushed

1 tablespoon tomato purée (paste)

salt to taste

Enough for 2 hungry people

Wash the fish and dry with kitchen paper. Cut into 4–5cm/1$\frac{1}{2}$–2in squares and set aside. Crush the garlic, ginger and salt to a paste.

Heat the oil gently in a large sauté pan (one that has a lid), add the garlic-ginger paste and cook for 1 minute. Add the curry powder, *dhana jiru*, chilli powder, turmeric, chillies and half of the coriander and stir around for about 30 seconds. Then add the crushed tomatoes, tomato purée and fried onions. Bring up to simmering point and cook until the onions start to break down and the oil pools around the sides of the pan.

Add 425ml/$\frac{3}{4}$ pint/1$\frac{2}{3}$ cups of water and bring to the boil. Taste the *masala* for salt and adjust. Then, with the heat low enough to maintain a gentle simmer, add the fish pieces. Turn them briefly in the sauce to coat them thoroughly, then cover and cook for 5 minutes or until the fish is opaque and flakes cleanly (timing depends on your choice of fish). Sprinkle with the remaining chopped coriander leaves and serve immediately.

Tandoori fish
Tandoori machi

The gutsy flavour of the *masala* in this recipe calls for dense-fleshed fish, which are coated and marinated in the spicy sauce, then roasted in the oven (you could also cook them on a barbecue). This gives a spicy crust and tender, juicy flesh beneath – cooking the fish whole helps keep it succulent. (If you'd prefer to eat fillets, make Spiced Fried Fish, on page 42, instead.) Prepare the fish the day before to give it time to absorb the seasonings in the marinade.

Put the whole roast fish proudly in the centre of the table with a pile of *naan* breads, some Lemon Salt Pickle (page 126) and salad leaves for a lively, sociable meal with friends.

2 whole fish such as tilapia, bream (porgy) or red snapper, gutted, scaled and cleaned, weighing about 1.35kg/3lb in total

FOR THE LEMON MARINADE

1 tablespoon lemon juice

1/2 teaspoon turmeric

2 teaspoons salt

FOR THE TANDOORI MASALA

6 cloves garlic, crushed with 1/2 teaspoon salt

2 tablespoons mild olive oil

2 tablespoons mustard oil

4 teaspoons *dhana jiru* (page 16)

1 teaspoon chilli powder

1/2 teaspoon turmeric

2 heaped tablespoons tomato purée (paste)

1/2 teaspoon *kasoori methi* (dried fenugreek leaves), crumbled

Lemon wedges to serve

To feed 4 generously

Wash the fish thoroughly, then dry with kitchen paper. In a wide, shallow dish large enough to hold the fish in a single layer if possible, mix the lemon juice, turmeric and salt. Lightly slash the fish diagonally across both sides and lay them in the dish, turning them to coat with the marinade. Cover with clingfilm (plastic wrap) and leave in the fridge for at least 2 hours.

Mix all the *tandoori masala* ingredients together in a bowl. When the fish has had a few hours in the lemon marinade, remove it from the fridge. Take 2 tablespoons of the lemon marinade mixture and add it to the *tandoori masala*. Drain the fish and discard the remaining marinade. Return the fish to the dish and, using your hands, coat the fish thickly and evenly with *tandoori masala* on both sides and inside the belly cavity, too. Cover the dish tightly with clingfilm and leave overnight in the fridge.

About 15 minutes before you want to cook, preheat your oven to its highest setting. Transfer the fish to a roasting pan and roast in the oven for 15 minutes. Remove the fish and baste well with the juices in the pan. Reduce the oven temperature to 200°C/400°F/gas mark 6 and cook for 15 minutes, then turn the fish over and cook for 10 minutes more. It should be crusty and a little charred in places, and the flesh should be opaque all the way to the bone. Serve hot with lemon wedges.

Masala fish and potatoes
Tareli machi ne masala vara bateta

Fish and chips, East African-Indian-style: in a rich, spicy sauce. The cooking technique is a little unusual – first, the fish and potatoes are fried, then they are added to a thick, spicy *masala* for a brief reheating – but the result is absolutely delicious. The fierce heat of the deep-frying sears the outside of the fish, whilst the flesh near the bone remains succulent. When we make this at home, we always have to add extra potatoes for my wife Salima (an addiction of hers); nevertheless, there are never enough.

   This dish is ideal for entertaining as most of the work – the frying – can be done well before guests are due to arrive. Rose uses a *karai* on the stove top and fries the fish and potatoes in small batches, but if you have a deep-fat fryer then use that – it's safer. Make sure you discard the oil afterwards; it will be tainted with the spices from the fish marinade. If you are using a wok or *karai* on the stove, do not fill it to more than a third of its depth, never leave it unattended and have a lid or spatter guard ready for when you add the fish – because it's wet from the marinade it can splutter a bit.

4 small or 2 large whole fish such as tilapia, snapper or bream (porgy), gutted, scaled and cleaned, or 6 steaks on the bone

Juice of 1 lemon

3 teaspoons salt

$\frac{1}{2}$ teaspoon turmeric

700g/1lb 9oz small potatoes (about 10), peeled and cut into 1cm-/$\frac{1}{2}$in-thick slices

Groundnut (peanut) oil for deep-frying

FOR THE MASALA

6 cloves garlic, crushed with 1 teaspoon salt

400g/14oz can plum tomatoes and juice, crushed

$2\frac{1}{2}$ teaspoons *dhana jiru* (page 16)

1 teaspoon chilli powder

$\frac{1}{2}$ teaspoon turmeric

2 tablespoons ready-fried onions (or 3 medium onions prepared as described on page 19)

1 tablespoon finely chopped coriander (cilantro) stems

1 tablespoon chopped coriander (cilantro) leaves

For 4 with chappatis

Remove and discard the fish heads (although Rose says they're the best bit). Cut each fish right through the body to make 2 pieces if using small fish, or 4 if using large fish. Place in a non-reactive dish, sprinkle with the lemon juice, salt and turmeric. Leave the fish to marinate for 20 minutes, turning now and again.

Fill a wok or *karai* with oil to a third of its depth and set over medium heat, or get your deep-fat fryer ready for frying, setting the thermostat to 160°C/325°F. When the oil is hot (a slice of potato should rise to the surface, suspended by bubbles), remove 2 or 4 pieces of fish from the marinade and shake off excess liquid. Lower the pieces carefully into the oil on a slotted spoon, standing well back. The oil will fizz and splutter, so have a lid or a spatter guard ready to shield yourself (or close the lid of your fryer before »

» lowering the basket). Cover and wait for the fierce bubbling to die down a bit. Turn the pieces gently to brown them evenly. Once the outside of the fish is golden-brown, remove to a plate lined with kitchen paper. Repeat with the remaining fish, frying in small batches to avoid overcrowding the pan.

Then lower the heat slightly (to 150°C/300°F for those using a deep-fat fryer) and cook the potatoes until golden, in two or three batches. Drain each batch on kitchen paper. Once all the frying is complete, turn off the heat.

When the pan is cool enough to handle, carefully pour the oil into a heatproof jug (pitcher) and wipe out the wok or *karai* with kitchen paper. Mix together all the *masala*

ingredients except for the coriander leaves. Put a tablespoon of the reserved oil back into the wok or *karai* (or into a clean one of you have used a deep-fat fryer) and set over medium-high heat. Add the *masala* mixture and cook rapidly until the onions begin to break down and the spice-tinted oil pools around the sides of the pan.

Reduce the heat to a gentle simmer and add the fish pieces. Turn them gently in the *masala*, taking care not to break the skin. Cook for a minute or so until just reheated.

Remove the fish to a warmed serving dish, then add the potatoes to the wok, tossing them to coat in the remaining *masala*, and warm through. Remove to the serving dish, sprinkle with the reserved coriander leaves and serve immediately.

Baked fish and rice
Machi bhath

Rose was taught how to cook this recipe by her mother-in-law: part of her initiation into the Hirani family was for Rose to learn all of her husband's family's favourite dishes. The Hiranis had rather different tastes to Rose's family, giving her an opportunity to dramatically expand her repertoire but, once the recipes were learned, Rose's own sense of taste and balance would take over. With time and repeated cooking, the dishes were refined and adapted as she saw fit. A prime example is in Rose's modification of this recipe: she doesn't include any of the whole spices that are normally used, resulting in a cleaner, fresher flavour than that of the original.

This dish is flavoursome and satisfying (the herby, zesty *masala* permeates both fish and rice wonderfully) and makes a complete meal served with just a little *Kachumber* (page 138) or Lemon Salt Pickle (page 126).

Serves 4

2 large whole fish such tilapia, snapper or bream (porgy), gutted, scaled and cleaned

Juice of 1 lemon

$1/2$ teaspoon turmeric

1 teaspoon salt

Groundnut (peanut) oil for deep-frying

1 quantity Spiced Roast Potatoes (page 89)*

FOR THE FENUGREEK PASTE

$1/2$ bunch of fenugreek (about 110g/4oz), leaves picked and stems discarded

Handful of coriander (cilantro) leaves

4 cloves garlic

2cm/1in ginger

$1^{1}/2$ teaspoons salt

3 green chillies

6 tomatoes cut into large pieces

FOR THE MASALA

4 medium onions, finely chopped

$1/2$ teaspoon *dhana jiru* (page 16)

$1/2$ teaspoon chilli powder

$1/2$ teaspoon turmeric

1 tablespoon lemon juice

FOR THE RICE

1 clove garlic, finely chopped

1cm/$1/2$in ginger, finely chopped

$1/8$ teaspoon turmeric

2 teaspoons salt

3 cups basmati rice

* *This item can be prepared while you marinate the fish; see notes in the method.*

First, marinate the fish. Remove the heads from the fish and discard (unless, of course, you'd like to cook and eat them). Cut each fish right through the body to make 4 pieces. Mix the lemon juice, turmeric and a teaspoon of salt in a non-reactive dish, add the fish pieces and leave to stand for 20 minutes or so.

Meanwhile, roast the potatoes as instructed on page 89. Once the potatoes are in the oven, make the fenugreek paste. Put the fenugreek and coriander leaves, garlic, ginger, chillies, salt and tomatoes into the bowl of a food processor. Blend to a fine paste and set aside. When the potatoes are done, remove them from the oven but leave it on – you'll need it later.

Fill a wok or *karai* with oil to a third of its depth and set over medium heat, or get your deep-fat fryer ready for frying, setting the thermostat to 160°C/325°F. When the oil is hot (a fragment of bread should rise to the surface, suspended by bubbles), remove 2 pieces of fish from the marinade and shake off excess liquid. Lower the pieces carefully into the oil on a slotted spoon, standing well back. The oil will fizz and splutter, so have a lid or a spatter guard ready to shield yourself (or close the lid of your fryer before lowering the basket). Cover and wait for the fierce bubbling to die down. Turn the pieces gently to brown them evenly. Once the outside of the fish is golden-brown, remove to a plate lined with kitchen paper. Repeat with the remaining fish, frying in small batches to avoid overcrowding the pan.

When all the fish is fried, carefully remove all but about 6 tablespoons of oil from the pan – reserve the rest in a heatproof jug (pitcher). Set aside 2 tablespoons of chopped onions and add the rest to the pan to make the *masala*. Fry the onions over medium heat until golden-brown. Then add the fenugreek paste, the *dhana jiru*, chilli powder and turmeric. Simmer until the oil pools around the sides of the pan, then stir in the lemon juice. Turn off the heat and set aside.

Now cook the rice. Put another 1½ tablespoons of the reserved oil in a large pot and place over medium heat. Add the reserved onions and fry until light golden-brown. Add the garlic and ginger and cook for a minute or so, then add 6 cups of water (use the same cup you used to measure out the rice), the turmeric and salt and bring to the boil. Take a tablespoon of the *masala* and add it to the boiling water. Add the rice, stir briefly and put on the lid. Boil for 7–10 minutes, until the rice is just cooked – tender, but retaining some bite. Then drain the rice in a colander or sieve.

Add the fried fish and roast potatoes to the *masala* and turn in the sauce to coat – take care not to break the fish skin. Put half the rice in the bottom of a casserole dish, then spread the fish and *masala* in a layer across the rice. Top with the remaining rice, then cover with a lid or tightly crimped foil. Turn the oven down to 170°C/325°F/gas mark 3, then put in the casserole dish. Cook until thoroughly warmed through – about 10 minutes – then serve.

Prawn curry
Soneya nu saak

Wonderful even if you use frozen prawns (shrimp), this punchy, deliciously spicy curry is a regular treat in our house. In fact, it is the jewel in the crown of our storecupboard standbys – with a bag of prawns in the freezer, you can make a curry quicker than you can say 'takeaway menu'. When you want something really good to eat, but don't want to spend too long cooking, this is perfect; it's so quickly rustled up, it feels like convenience food – but the flavour is complex, satisfying and special enough to serve to guests. On such occasions, splash out and buy fresh jumbo king prawns. They will not disappoint, retaining their succulence and flavour well in this delicious, rich *masala*.

325g/11oz peeled cooked prawns (shrimp), thoroughly defrosted if frozen

3 tablespoons groundnut (peanut) oil

1 small onion, very finely chopped

3 cloves garlic, crushed with $\frac{1}{2}$ teaspoon salt

$\frac{1}{2}$ teaspoon Madras curry powder

1 teaspoon *dhana jiru* (page 16)

$\frac{1}{2}$ teaspoon chilli powder

$\frac{1}{2}$ teaspoon turmeric

200ml/7fl oz crushed canned plum tomatoes and juice (about half a can)

1 tablespoon tomato purée (paste)

$\frac{1}{2}$ tablespoon finely chopped coriander (cilantro) stems

$\frac{1}{2}$ tablespoon roughly chopped or torn coriander (cilantro) leaves

Serves 2 with chappatis

First, wash the prawns. Remove the dark vein running along the back of larger ones by making a light incision and scraping it away. Then dry the prawns, pressing them gently between sheets of kitchen paper to extract excess moisture. It is important to do this thoroughly; if the prawns are too wet, you'll end up with a rather sloppy result. Once dry, bundle them up in some kitchen paper and place in a bowl in the fridge while you make the *masala*.

Heat the oil in a medium-sized pan and fry the onion over a gentle heat until golden-brown. This will take about 10 minutes – keep the heat lowish and stir regularly to cook the onion evenly. (Don't be tempted to do this over a high heat to speed things up – the onion will burn, or at least cook less evenly, and the resulting flavour just won't be as good.)

When the onion is golden-brown, add the garlic paste and spices. Cook for a few seconds, then add 3 tablespoons of water and cook gently until reduced to a slushy paste. Add the tomatoes, tomato purée and coriander stems, increase the heat and simmer, stirring frequently, until the oil pools around the sides of the pan.

Add the prawns and cook gently for a few minutes until they are heated through – the size of prawns you have will dictate how long they need. Don't overdo it or the prawns will toughen. Serve immediately, sprinkled with the coriander leaves.

Meat

A potent symbol of well-being and generosity, meat is held in the highest regard in Muslim culture. Unsurprisingly, recipes for meat are legion – this chapter is merely a cross-section of dishes that we find ourselves returning to again and again. Many of these recipes come from my late father-in-law's side of the family – make no mistake, the Hiranis love their meat! Over the years, with their expert guidance, Rose has become as proficient in cooking the Hiranis' favourite meat dishes as she is with the vegetable dishes she has cooked since childhood. In Africa, the meat the family ate was not produced intensively – it came from local, small-scale farmers. Rose missed the lovely flavour of that meat when she came to the UK in the early 1970s but, now that organic meat is widely available, we've switched to using this exclusively in our cooking: Rose says it reminds her of the delicious meat she ate in Africa. With flavour in mind, our recipes call for bone to be retained when meat is cut into pieces. This can be tricky to achieve at home: your best bet is to befriend your local butcher and ask him to cut up the bones as he makes up your order of meat.

TO COMPLEMENT MEAT, sweet spices such as cloves, cinnamon, cardamom and peppercorns are often used. Although Rose finds them too overbearing to use with the more delicate flavours of vegetables and fish, with meat they work a special magic, enhancing its savouriness and rich texture wonderfully. Sometimes used whole, and sometimes roasted and ground in the form of *garam masala* (see our recipe on page 16), they add a warm, fragrant and rather special note to meat dishes.

Lamb curry
Ghosh nu saak

For this, the most basic of the meat curries in this book, it is more important than ever that the meat you use is of the best quality. The resulting curry will be rich, deeply savoury and satisfying; pair with basmati rice for a simple, perfect meal.

TO COOK THE MEAT

450g/1lb lamb from the shoulder or leg, cut into 5cm/2in pieces with bone retained, trimmed of fat and rinsed to remove stray splinters of bone

2 cloves garlic

1cm/½in ginger

FOR THE MASALA

4 cloves garlic

2.5cm/1in ginger

½ teaspoon salt

4 tablespoons groundnut (peanut) oil

2 small onions (or 1 large), finely chopped

1 teaspoon Madras curry powder

1 teaspoon *dhana jiru* (page 16)

½ teaspoon chilli powder

½ teaspoon turmeric

1 teaspoon finely chopped coriander (cilantro) stems

200ml/7fl oz crushed canned plum tomatoes and juice (about half a can)

1 tablespoon tomato purée (paste)

TO FINISH

2 potatoes, peeled and halved

½ teaspoon *garam masala* (page 16)

1 tablespoon chopped coriander (cilantro) leaves

Serves 2–3 people

Put the meat in a medium-sized pan. Crush the garlic and ginger to a paste and add to the pan with 325ml/12fl oz/1½ cups of water. Bring to the boil, simmer rapidly for 10 minutes, then reduce the heat and cover. Cook until the meat is tender – about 45 minutes to an hour.

Meanwhile, make the *masala*. Crush the garlic and ginger to a paste with the salt and set aside. In a large pan, heat the oil and add the onions. Fry over medium heat, stirring often to prevent the onions from burning. When they're golden-brown, reduce the heat and add the curry powder, *dhana jiru*, chilli powder and turmeric. Reserve ½ teaspoon of the garlic-ginger paste for use later – put the remaining paste into the pan with the onions and spices. Cook for a few seconds, then add 250ml/8fl oz/1 cup of water and the coriander stems. Bring up to simmering point and cook rapidly until the onions begin to break down. Add the tomatoes and tomato purée. Stir well, bring up to simmering point and cook until the *masala* is thick and oil pools around the sides of the pan.

Skim and discard any fat from the meat cooking water, then add meat and water to the *masala*. Throw in the potatoes and give everything a good stir around. Add 500ml/18fl oz/2 cups more water, and the reserved portion of garlic-ginger paste. Bring to the boil, reduce the heat to a simmer, then cover and cook until the potatoes are tender. Stir in the *garam masala*, sprinkle with the coriander leaves and serve.

Lamb with dal
Ghosh vari daar

This flavoursome, economical dish was a firm favourite of my late father-in-law. He would happily eat this humble lentil-thickened stew every day if Rose offered it to him. It's a perfect meal for cold days – spiked with ginger and chilli, it is warming and filling – and any leftovers will be even better the next day because the flavours have more time to infuse.

225g/8oz/1 cup *channa dal* (split chickpeas), well rinsed

2 tablespoons *moong dal*, well rinsed

450g/1lb lamb from the shoulder or leg, cubed with bone retained, trimmed of fat and rinsed to remove stray splinters of bone

1½ teaspoons salt

3 fat cloves garlic

3cm/1½in ginger

4 green chillies

½ teaspoon cumin seeds

2 tablespoons groundnut (peanut) oil

1 medium onion, finely chopped

2.5cm/1in cinnamon stick

3 cardamoms

3 cloves

10 peppercorns

4 tablespoons crushed canned plum tomatoes and juice

¼ teaspoon turmeric

½ tablespoon finely chopped coriander (cilantro) stems

2 medium potatoes, peeled and halved

Juice of half a lemon

½ tablespoon chopped coriander (cilantro) leaves

Serves 4 people with rice or chappatis

Put both types of *dal* in a small pan with 1 litre/1¾ pints/4 cups of water and bring to the boil. Skim off any scum, then partially cover the pan and simmer until the pulses are soft. This should take about 30 minutes – you may need to add more boiling water from time to time.

Meanwhile, put the meat in a small pan with 500ml/18fl oz/2 cups of water and ½ teaspoon of the salt. Bring to the boil, skim off any scum and cook rapidly for 10 minutes. Reduce the heat and simmer for about 45 minutes until tender.

Crush the garlic, ginger, 2 of the chillies, cumin seeds and 1 teaspoon of salt to a paste. Set aside.

Heat the oil in a large pan and add the onion, cinnamon, cardamoms, cloves and peppercorns. Cook over moderate heat until the edges of the onion begin to turn brown. Add the garlic-ginger paste and cook for a minute or so, then add the tomatoes, the remaining 2 green chillies (left whole), turmeric, coriander stems and the potatoes. Stir well and simmer until the oil pools around the sides of the pan.

Add the cooked meat and its cooking liquid to the *masala* and continue to cook over medium heat. Purée the *dal* and its cooking water using a hand-held blender, or beat with a whisk – it should be fairly thin and soupy. Add it to the *masala*. Simmer gently until the potatoes are tender. When you're ready to serve, stir in the lemon juice and chopped coriander and check the seasoning, adding more salt if necessary.

Spiced roast lamb
Sekelu ghosh

In simple terms this is roast leg of lamb with an Indian twist. A rich marinade flavours and tenderises the meat, cooking down to a tasty crust and thickened *masala* to serve alongside the roast. It's great for a party – the lamb leg looks bountiful and celebratory and is delicious hot or cold. And it couldn't be simpler to prepare: it's just a matter of marinating the lamb the night before, then roasting it for three hours or so, with little further attention required. Present the joint proudly on a large platter, letting guests carve their own servings to eat with warm pitta bread or *naan*, salad leaves, *Raitha* (page 130) and some of the sauce. As you would expect, roast potatoes make a good accompaniment, especially the Spiced Roast Potatoes on page 89.

1 leg of lamb, weighing about 1.6kg/3½lb
8 cloves garlic
7.5cm/3in ginger
1 teaspoon salt
3 tablespoons yoghurt
3 tablespoons groundnut (peanut) oil
275ml/10fl oz crushed canned plum tomatoes and juice (about two-thirds of a can)
1 teaspoon chilli powder
½ teaspoon turmeric

For 6–8 people (or more as part of a buffet)

Put the lamb in a deep, non-reactive dish. Take a sharp knife and stab the meat deeply all over – this will help the marinade permeate the meat. Crush the garlic and ginger with the salt to a

paste. Mix with the yoghurt, oil, tomatoes, chilli powder and turmeric and stir well. Pour the marinade over the meat, rubbing it in well and turning the meat to coat all over. Cover the dish with clingfilm (plastic wrap) and place in the fridge for at least 8 hours or overnight if possible, turning the meat from time to time.

About an hour before you want to cook the lamb, remove it from the fridge to allow it to come up to room temperature. Then, about 20 minutes before you intend to cook, preheat the oven to 210°C/425°F/gas mark 7.

Put the meat in a roasting pan, pour in the marinade and turn the meat to coat it well with the marinade. Cover the pan with foil, leaving a small corner open to allow steam to escape. Place in the oven and roast for 30 minutes, then reduce the heat to 180°C/350°F/gas mark 4.

After about 1½ hours, remove the foil, baste the meat with the marinade in the pan and return to the oven. Cook until the meat is tender (test by piercing the thickest part of the meat with a skewer – if the juices that run out are clear, the meat is done). This will take about 1 more hour. If you feel the meat is browning too much, cover it with foil again and continue cooking.

When the meat is done, remove it from the oven and place on a warmed platter. Cover it with foil and let it rest for around 30 minutes before carving – this will ensure juicy, tender meat. Avoiding pools of excess fat, scoop any remaining marinade from the pan into a bowl and keep warm, to serve alongside the joint.

Lamb with saffron and yoghurt
Kalyo

Tender meat in a velvety sauce of yoghurt and fried onions, highly scented with sweet spices, *Kalyo* isn't quick to cook – but it's well worth the effort. You need to marinate the meat the night before for best results. Serve with *Naan* (page 114) or *Varela Parotha* (page 118).

900g/2lb lamb from the shoulder or leg, cut into 3cm/1½in chunks with bone retained, rinsed to remove stray splinters of bone
1 quantity Spiced Roast Potatoes (page 89)*
3 tablespoons ready-fried onions (or 4 medium onions prepared as described on page 19*)

FOR THE MARINADE

5 cloves garlic
6cm/2½in ginger
1 teaspoon salt
About 25 saffron strands
125ml/4fl oz/½ cup yoghurt
1cm/½in cinnamon stick
3 cardamoms
3 cloves
8 peppercorns
8 tablespoons crushed canned plum tomatoes and juice
¾ teaspoon chilli powder

FOR THE VAGAR

2 fat cloves garlic
2cm/1in ginger
50g/2oz/¼ cup butter
½ teaspoon *garam masala* (page 16)

* These items can be prepared while you cook the lamb; see notes in the method.

For 4–6 people with breads

Put the meat in a non-reactive mixing bowl. Crush the garlic, ginger and salt to a paste and add to the meat with the remaining marinade ingredients. Stir well, cover the bowl with clingfilm (plastic wrap) and leave overnight in the fridge. About an hour before you intend to cook the meat, remove it from the refrigerator to allow it to come up to room temperature.

Put meat and marinade in a large pan over high heat. Bring the mixture to the boil and cook rapidly, uncovered, for 10 minutes. Reduce the heat to a simmer, cover the pan and cook for about 1 hour until the meat is very tender. Meanwhile, roast your potatoes and fry your onions (if you're not using ready-fried).

When the meat is cooked, remove and discard the whole spices. Add the roast potatoes to the pan and enough hot water to entirely cover the meat and potatoes – then 250ml/8fl oz/1 cup for good measure. Add the fried onions and bring up to the boil. Simmer for 10 minutes to thicken the *masala*, stirring periodically.

Just before serving, make the *vagar*. Crush the garlic and ginger to a paste. Heat the butter in a small pan and, when it foams, add the garlic-ginger paste and the *garam masala*. Stir constantly for a minute or so until the garlic turns golden, then tip the *vagar* over the curry, stir well, cook for a couple of minutes and serve.

Minced lamb with peas
Kheema mattar nu saak

Use the best, leanest minced (ground) lamb you can find for this curry and you'll be rewarded with a rich velvety sauce. Sweet peas are a lovely counterpoint to the savoury meat. This has always been a weekday curry in Rose's house, served with *Rotli* (page 108) and a little *dal* and rice, but if you want to make it a little more special, serve with *Varela Parotha* (page 118).

2 tablespoons groundnut (peanut) oil

4cm/1½in cinnamon stick

1 clove

1 cardamom

3 peppercorns

2 medium onions, finely chopped

3 fat cloves garlic

4cm/1½in ginger

½ teaspoon salt

500g/1lb lean minced (ground) lamb

½ teaspoon Madras curry powder

1½ teaspoons *dhana jiru* (page 16)

¼ teaspoon chilli powder

¼ teaspoon turmeric

½ tablespoon finely chopped coriander (cilantro) stems

1 fresh red chilli, halved (and deseeded if you don't want too much heat)

¼ teaspoon paprika

200ml/7fl oz crushed canned plum tomatoes and juice (about half a can)

2 medium potatoes

150g/6oz/1½ cups frozen peas

¼ teaspoon *garam masala* (page 16)

1 tablespoon chopped coriander (cilantro) leaves

Serves 2 with breads, or more if served as part of a larger meal

Heat the oil in a large pan and add the cinnamon, cardamom, clove, peppercorns and the onions. Cook gently for about 10 minutes until the onions are golden-brown, stirring frequently. In the meantime, crush the garlic, ginger and salt to a paste and set aside.

When the onions are nicely browned, add the lamb, curry powder, *dhana jiru*, chilli powder and turmeric and stir well. Break up any lumps so that the meat can brown evenly. When the meat is browned, add the coriander stems, red chilli, garlic-ginger paste and paprika. Stir-fry for another 10 minutes, then add the tomatoes. Simmer for 10 minutes, stirring frequently (if you find the mixture sticks to the pan, add 2–3 tablespoons of water).

Peel the potatoes and cut into 2cm/1in cubes. Add them and 125ml/4fl oz/½ cup of water to the pan. Stir well, cover and cook for about 15 minutes until the potatoes are almost done. Add the peas and simmer until they are just cooked. Add the *garam masala*, stir well, then sprinkle with coriander leaves and serve.

Meatball curry
Kabab nu saak

Almost 20 years after giving up meat, my wife says she still remembers, with fond nostalgia, how this curry tastes. No wonder: the rich *masala* and spicy, melting meatballs are sublime.

FOR THE MEATBALLS

450g/1lb lean minced (ground) lamb

2 cloves garlic

2 green chillies

¼ teaspoon salt

Juice of half a lemon

½ teaspoon *dhana jiru* (page 16)

¼ teaspoon turmeric

¼ teaspoon ground cumin

1 medium onion, peeled and grated

½ tablespoon finely chopped coriander (cilantro) leaves

FOR THE MASALA

4 cloves garlic

1cm/½in ginger

¼ teaspoon salt

3 tablespoons groundnut (peanut) oil

2 small onions, finely chopped

1 teaspoon Madras curry powder

1 teaspoon *dhana jiru* (page 16)

¼ teaspoon chilli powder

½ teaspoon turmeric

1 tablespoon finely chopped coriander (cilantro) stems

1 fresh red chilli

200ml/7fl oz crushed canned plum tomatoes and juice (about half a can)

½ tablespoon tomato purée (paste)

½ tablespoon chopped coriander (cilantro) leaves

For 4 with rice or chappatis

To make the meatballs, put the lamb in a large bowl. Pound the garlic, chillies and salt to a paste. Add it and all the remaining meatball ingredients to the lamb and mix thoroughly. Shape into golf-ball-sized meatballs, firming them together well (you'll end up with 15 or so).

For the *masala*, crush the garlic, ginger and salt to a paste. Heat the oil in a wide pan (large enough to hold the meatballs in a single layer). Add the onions and fry over medium heat, stirring frequently, until golden-brown. Add the garlic-ginger paste, curry powder, *dhana jiru*, chilli powder and turmeric. Cook for 30 seconds, then add 250ml/8fl oz/1 cup of water, the chilli, coriander stems, canned tomatoes and tomato purée. Stir and bring up to a simmer. Cook until the oil pools around the sides of the pan.

Add the meatballs to the pan in a single layer. Reduce the heat to a simmer and gently shake the pan to settle the meatballs into the *masala*. Do NOT move the meatballs, or they will break. Cover and cook for 10 minutes. Remove the lid and stir the meatballs around gently to coat them in the *masala* – they'll have become quite firm now. Cook until the meatballs are done – around 10 minutes (break a meatball open to see if it is cooked through – if it's still pink inside, cook for about 5 minutes more). Serve as it is with chappatis, or add 570ml/1 pint/2 cups of water to the pan, bring to the boil and simmer for a few minutes before serving with boiled basmati rice. Scatter with the chopped coriander leaves before you take the curry to the table.

Minced lamb kebabs
Shish kabab

These spicy, juicy and deeply savoury kebabs are perfect barbecue fare because they're entirely foolproof and stress-free. Precooking the kebabs in the oven ensures they don't break up on the grill (and no one gets anything undercooked).

You'll need some skewers to hand – the best I've found are flat metal ones. They make the process of turning the kebabs easier as the meat doesn't spin round, but you can use any skewers that are around 20cm/8in in length. If you use bamboo skewers, remember to soak them in hot water for half an hour before you assemble the kebabs, to stop them burning.

Serve with *Rotli* (page 108), *Naan* (page 114) or pittas, a finely sliced *Kachumber* (page 138), Coriander Chutney (page 132) and yoghurt.

450g/1lb lean minced (ground) lamb

4 cloves garlic

3cm/1½in ginger, roughly chopped

3 green chillies, roughly chopped

½ teaspoon cumin seeds

1 teaspoon salt

1 medium onion, grated

4 tablespoons finely chopped coriander (cilantro) leaves

Scant teaspoon *kasoori methi* (dried fenugreek leaves), rinsed and drained in a sieve

Large pinch of turmeric

½ teaspoon salt

½ teaspoon *garam masala* (page 16)

Makes 12–14 kebabs, depending on the size of your skewers

Place the meat in a large mixing bowl. Crush the garlic, ginger, chillies, cumin seeds and salt to a paste. Add the mixture to the lamb, along with the remaining ingredients. Mix thoroughly (the best way to do this is by hand, to ensure thorough, even mixing).

Line a baking tray (pan) large enough to hold the kebabs with greaseproof (waxed) paper.

With wet hands, shape the mixture into sausages that are short enough to fit on your skewers, roughly 2cm/1in in thickness. Slide the skewers into the sausages and squeeze the meat firmly around them. Lay the kebabs on the paper-lined tray as you proceed.

If possible, chill the kebabs for 2–3 hours to give them a chance to firm up. Preheat the oven to 200°C/400°F/gas mark 6. Put the tray of kebabs in the oven and cook for 10 minutes only. When you're ready to eat, preheat your grill (broiler) or barbecue, and brown the kebabs to your liking.

KIDS LOVE THESE KEBABS – we always make a separate batch without chillies for young guests, making them into smaller, fun-size kebabs to distinguish them from the adults' *tikha* (spicy-hot) ones.

Barbecue marinade
Mishkaki

My late father-in-law, Madat, was a barbecue enthusiast. It appealed to his sociable nature to hold impromptu, sizeable gatherings of family and friends, with *mishkaki* as the central focus. Many of the family remember these occasions, and the food served at them, with fondness. Guests would bring their own barbecues and the garden would be transformed into a cook-out. Rose would prepare a little bread and salad and, for once, sit back while her husband did the real cooking. It was the only dish he ever cooked – but over the years he became an expert. Sadly, I didn't get a chance to ask him for his wisdom on the cooking of meat on an outdoor grill (my notes below are common sense only), but Rose can pass on his much-loved marinade recipe.

This concoction works brilliantly with cubed lamb (threaded onto skewers for grilling), chops, cutlets, butterflied leg of lamb and chicken – particularly wings. The kiwi fruit may seem strange, but it's an effective meat tenderiser, reducing the marinating time to just a couple of hours. Remember, though, that it must be left out if you plan to marinate overnight, or if you are using chicken – it's just too potent!

4 cloves garlic
3cm/1½in ginger
4 green chillies
2 teaspoons salt
2 kiwi fruit, peeled and cut into large chunks (use only for quick-marinating lamb)
1 generous tablespoon yoghurt
¼ teaspoon turmeric
1 tablespoon groundnut (peanut) oil

Enough for about 1kg/2lb lamb or chicken, to serve 4 people with bread and salad leaves

For quick-marinating lamb cubes, steaks, chops or cutlets, combine all the marinade ingredients in a large, non-reactive bowl. Add the meat and stir thoroughly. Cover and leave in the fridge for no more than 2 hours. When you are ready to cook, remove the kiwi pieces and discard them. If you are using cubed lamb, thread onto skewers. Brush the meat generously with the marinade, then grill to your liking.

For butterflied leg of lamb, follow the directions above, but rub the marinade all over the lamb before leaving to marinate for 2 hours.

For chicken pieces, mix the marinade ingredients, except for the kiwi, then add the chicken. Marinate for 1 hour only. Grill until thoroughly cooked.

For overnight marinating of lamb (chicken is too tender for this treatment), remember to omit the kiwi fruit.

To prepare your barbecue for cooking, light the coals a good half-hour before you intend to cook. Allow all flames to die down and, when the coals are glowing under a light coating of grey ash, you're ready to start cooking. It's very important to remember that chicken should be thoroughly cooked – the meat should be opaque throughout (be sure to check close to the bone) and, when the meat is pierced with a skewer, the juices that run out should be absolutely clear, with no traces of pink.

Chicken shish kebabs
Kukra ni shish kabab

Using organic free-range chicken will make all the difference in this recipe. It will have a far superior flavour and texture, of course, with the added benefit that the meat will not shrink during cooking. Nor will it exude any water while it cooks, so the kebabs are less likely to fall apart. It can be tricky to track down good minced (ground) chicken – we tend to buy a whole chicken and bone and mince (grind) it ourselves. It is worth it: these are tasty and moreish – when we tested the recipe for this book, Rose and I polished off the whole lot in one sitting – but we reckon the recipe would feed four (normal) people, with freshly made *Naan* (page 114), crisp salad leaves and Tamarind Chutney (page 133).

450g/1lb minced (ground) chicken

3 cloves garlic

5cm/2in ginger

2 green chillies, topped and tailed, and split

$\frac{1}{2}$ teaspoon cumin seeds

$1\frac{1}{2}$ teaspoons salt

$\frac{1}{2}$ red chilli, deseeded and finely chopped

2 spring onions (scallions), finely sliced

$\frac{1}{4}$ red pepper, deseeded and finely chopped

$\frac{1}{2}$ teaspoon Madras curry powder

$\frac{1}{2}$ teaspoon *garam masala* (page 16)

$\frac{1}{2}$ tablespoon finely chopped coriander (cilantro) stems

1 tablespoon finely chopped coriander (cilantro) leaves

2 tablespoons groundnut (peanut) oil

Makes about 12 kebabs, depending on the size of your skewers

Have your skewers ready – if you're using bamboo ones, soak them for half an hour in warm water before you begin. Line a couple of baking trays (pans) with greaseproof (waxed) paper and set aside. Preheat the oven to 220°C/425°F/gas mark 7.

Put the chicken in a large mixing bowl. Pound the garlic, ginger, green chillies, cumin seeds and salt to a paste. Add the paste to the chicken with the other ingredients and mix well by hand.

Using wet hands, mould the mixture into sausage shapes, of a length that will fit comfortably onto your skewers. Don't make them too thick – about 2cm/¾in is thick enough. This will be a bit of a messy job – the chicken mixture is quite sticky – but persevere. Once the sausages are formed, slide the skewers inside. Firm the sausages around the skewers and neaten their shape, then place them on the paper-lined tray.

Cook the kebabs in the preheated oven for 5 minutes only. (You can do this stage in advance if you want – after their time in the oven, allow to cool completely, then cover and refrigerate.) When you're ready to eat, grill (broil) or barbecue them until they're golden-brown and cooked through (check by breaking a kebab open – the meat should be opaque all the way to the centre, with clear juices).

Chicken curry
Kukra nu saak

For me, this deceptively simple recipe makes the best chicken curry in the world: when I first tasted it, I thought I'd died and gone to heaven. A whole chicken is jointed and added with its bones to the cooking *masala*, bringing richness and depth to the finished sauce. Don't be tempted to use boneless chicken breast; this will not give the flavour or texture that using the whole bird, bones and all, does. Cooking the curry in this way effectively produces a chicken stock to enrich the sauce – and cooking the meat on the bone makes it very succulent.

1.8kg/4lb chicken, jointed (or the same weight of chicken pieces), skinned and breasts halved

3 tablespoons groundnut (peanut) oil

10cm/4in cinnamon stick, broken into 2 pieces

4 small onions, quartered and thinly sliced

3 fat cloves garlic

4cm/1½in ginger

1 teaspoon salt

½ tablespoon finely chopped coriander (cilantro) stems

¼ teaspoon Madras curry powder

2 teaspoons *dhana jiru* (page 16)

1 teaspoon chilli powder

½ teaspoon turmeric

400g/14oz can plum tomatoes and juice, crushed

2 teaspoons tomato purée (paste)

4 medium potatoes, peeled and halved

1 teaspoon *garam masala* (page 16)

1 tablespoon chopped coriander (cilantro) leaves

Serves 4 with rice

Wash the chicken pieces and pat dry with kitchen paper. Set aside. Put the oil in a large pan and warm over a medium heat until the oil is shimmering. Add the cinnamon sticks and onions. Reduce the heat to low and slowly fry the onions until they are golden-brown, stirring frequently to prevent the onions around the edges of the pan burning.

Meanwhile, crush the garlic, ginger and salt to a paste. When the onions are golden, add the garlic-ginger paste, the coriander stems, curry powder, *dhana jiru*, chilli powder and turmeric and cook for 30 seconds. Then add the tomatoes and tomato purée, increase the heat and cook until the oil pools around the sides of the pan.

Add the chicken and stir around to coat the pieces. Cook like this for 5 minutes, then add approximately 570ml/1 pint/2 cups of water (enough to come halfway up the chicken). Bring to the boil and add the potatoes. Cover and cook for about 20 minutes, until the chicken is thoroughly cooked and the potatoes are tender, but not breaking up. Add the *garam masala* and the chopped coriander, then taste and adjust the seasoning if necessary. Cook for a few minutes to meld the flavours, then serve.

AN ORGANIC CHICKEN will yield the best results; the inferior quality of the bones of a factory-farmed bird will not give the same depth and body to the finished *masala*.

Chicken with coconut
Kuku paka

Originating in coastal East Africa, where coconuts are abundant, this dish has been adopted and, typically, modified by the Indian migrant community (it's now a classic of East African-Indian cooking). Rose has tried many versions of *kuku paka*, but her favourite comes from her elder sister-in-law Zubeda. It's unlike any other dish in this book – the *masala* is made with coconut rather than tomatoes, and very little spice is used (although chillies do add a nice kick). Serve with crusty white bread for real authenticity, or rice, to mop up the rich sauce.

....

1.35kg/3lb chicken, jointed (or the same weight of chicken pieces), skinned and breasts halved
5 fat cloves garlic
5cm/2in ginger
250g/9oz block creamed coconut
5 green chillies
1 medium onion, roughly chopped
2 fresh tomatoes, peeled and roughly chopped
Scant $\frac{1}{2}$ teaspoon turmeric
1 teaspoon salt
4 medium potatoes, peeled and halved
Juice of 1 lemon
4 eggs, boiled for 8 minutes, cooled and shelled
1 tablespoon chopped coriander (cilantro)
Lemon or lime wedges to serve

Serves 4

....

Wash the chicken pieces and pat dry with kitchen paper. Set aside. Crush the garlic and ginger to a paste. Remove the coconut block from the packaging. At one end there is usually a small strip of more translucent, oilier coconut. Slice it off and discard, then chop the rest into rough chunks and throw them into a blender. Add 1.2 litres/2 pints/4$\frac{1}{2}$ cups of boiling water and blend until the coconut is dissolved. Pour the mixture through a sieve. Scrape what remains in the sieve back into the blender and add 250ml/8fl oz/1 cup of hot water. Blend, then strain again. Discard what remains in the sieve.

Rinse out the blender, then add the chillies, onion and tomatoes and blend well. If the mixture sticks, add 125ml/4fl oz/$\frac{1}{2}$ cup of water. Stir the resulting paste into the coconut milk.

Put the chicken, garlic-ginger paste, turmeric and salt into a large pan. Place over high heat and bring to the boil. Simmer rapidly until the liquid has reduced to half its original volume. Reduce the heat to a gentle simmer, cover and cook for 15 minutes. Add the potatoes, stir well, cover again and cook for roughly 15 minutes more, until the potatoes are about half cooked.

Add the coconut mixture and 250ml/8fl oz/1 cup of water. Stir constantly now (otherwise the coconut milk will separate) until the mixture boils, then reduce the heat to low and cook gently without the lid for about 15 minutes, until the potatoes and chicken are cooked. Add the boiled eggs in the last few minutes of cooking to heat them through.

Add lemon juice and salt to taste. To eat with rice, thin the sauce with some hot water – about 325ml/12fl oz/1$\frac{1}{2}$ cups. Sprinkle with the coriander and serve with lemon or lime wedges.

Cumin-fried chicken
Jira chicken

Tempting spice-crusted nuggets of chicken are good for parties or picnics, or for munching in front of a good movie. For best results, use chicken pieces on the bone, but you can use boneless thighs and breasts if you prefer (although they will be less succulent). Serve the chicken on a big platter, with salad leaves and *Raitha* (page 130) alongside – and I like mine with lime wedges to squeeze over. Provide napkins and eat the nuggets with your fingers.

1.35kg/3lb chicken, jointed and skinned (or use the same weight of chicken pieces)
5 teaspoons cumin seeds
3 cloves garlic
5cm/2in ginger
3 green chillies
1 teaspoon salt
2 tablespoons yoghurt
50g/2oz/¼ cup butter
1 tablespoon groundnut (peanut) oil
Lime wedges to serve (optional)

Serves 4 as a snack

Using a cleaver if you have one, chop the skinned chicken pieces into large nuggets (chopping through the bone as cleanly as possible). Chop the thighs and drumsticks into 2 pieces each, the breast into 4 and the wings into 2. (If you're on good terms with your butcher, you could ask him to do all of this for you.) Then wash the chicken to rinse away any splinters of bone, pat the pieces dry with kitchen paper and set them aside.

Crush the cumin seeds using a pestle and mortar – they don't need to be too fine.

Pound the garlic, ginger, chillies and salt to a paste, then add the yoghurt and half the crushed cumin seeds. Combine this marinade with the chicken in a non-reactive bowl. Leave for at least 20 minutes and up to 1 hour to marinate.

Then, heat the oil and butter in a large sauté pan (skillet). Over high heat, add half the remaining cumin seeds and cook until they are fragrant. Then add the chicken and marinade.

Bring up to the boil and simmer rapidly to reduce the liquid. When just a thin layer of liquid covers the base of the pan, add the remaining cumin and reduce the heat slightly.

Cook until the marinade is almost gone, then increase the heat to brown the chicken. Stir from time to time, scraping up any sticky bits, until the chicken is patched with golden-brown and thoroughly cooked. Check by prising some meat away from the bone – if it is completely opaque and any juices are clear, then it's done.

Serve piled up on a warm dish, with lime wedges if you like.

Tandoori chicken
Tandoori chicken

Our recipe for this ubiquitous dish lacks the vivid colour of its restaurant equivalent because we see no need to add nasty chemical food colouring. Tomato purée (paste) and turmeric give the chicken a natural, attractive appearance. (Personally, I find the lurid colour of restaurant tandoori offputting – I can never quite forget seeing a sketch on TV, from the British-Asian comedy show *Goodness Gracious Me!*, where a chef was seen, in the privacy of his restaurant kitchen, furtively dipping chicken pieces into orange paint.) But the taste of this dish is reassuringly familiar – gutsy, spicy and full-flavoured – thanks to *tandoori masala*. You'll find this spice blend in supermarkets and Indian grocers; check the ingredients don't include any artificial colourings. Prepare the chicken the night before you want to eat it, to allow the marinade to work its magic. Serve with *Naan* (page 114), *Raitha* (page 130) and salad leaves.

10 chicken pieces on the bone – a combination of drumsticks, thighs and breasts, as you like

6 cloves garlic

5cm/2in ginger

1/2 teaspoon salt

1/2 –1 teaspoon chilli powder, to taste

1/2 teaspoon turmeric

2 teaspoons *tandoori masala*

3 tablespoons yoghurt

1 tablespoon *kasoori methi* (dried fenugreek leaves)

1 1/2 tablespoons tomato purée (paste)

3 tablespoons groundnut (peanut) oil

Lemon wedges to serve

Enough for 4 greedy people

Skin the chicken pieces, wash them and pat dry with kitchen paper. Slash the thicker parts of the meat halfway through, to allow the marinade to penetrate, and set aside.

Pound the garlic, ginger and salt to a paste. Put it in a large, non-reactive bowl and add the remaining ingredients to make a thick spice paste. Add the chicken pieces, coating them well with the paste, then cover the bowl and leave in the fridge overnight.

About 2 hours before you want to cook, remove the chicken from the fridge and allow it to come up to room temperature. About 20 minutes before you intend to cook, preheat your oven to its highest setting.

Lay the chicken pieces on a baking tray (pan), making sure they are well coated with tandoori paste. Put them in the oven and roast for 15 minutes, then reduce the temperature to 200°C/400°F/gas mark 6. Cook until the chicken is thoroughly done, making sure the meat near the bones is opaque and any juices are clear. Serve hot, with lemon wedges.

Rice

Asserting his individuality in a family of committed bread eaters, Rose's father Karim insisted on at least a small amount of rice being served at every meal. His preference became family tradition, and this selection of his daughter's dishes demonstrates the versatility of rice – from the simplest preparations intended to provide a comforting foil and soak up a rich *masala*, to dishes that constitute a complete meal. There are everyday recipes such as *khichri* and some elaborate, celebratory ones such as *akhni*. Some rely on the delicate, aromatic character of rice – the scent of cooking basmati will surely make your mouth water – while others exploit the grain's ability to absorb flavours such as woody spices and intense aromatics. The Hindu vegetarian tradition of Rose's distant ancestors is apparent in some recipes; in them you'll find rice and pulses combined to create a protein of a nutritional quality comparable to meat. Many generations after the family's conversion to Islam, these dishes have endured, to rub shoulders with unmistakably Muslim dishes characterised by rich, elaborate spicing.

ROSE NEVER WEIGHS RICE; she says the simplest way to measure rice (and the correct amount of water needed to cook it) is to use a cup. Any cup will do, as long as you use the same one to measure both rice and water. One cup holds roughly enough rice for one person, but cup sizes and appetites vary. With a little trial and error you'll find a cup in your kitchen that works best for you.

Perfumed rice with moong dal
Chuthi khichri

Paired with Spiced Buttermilk (page 76), this forms the classic dish *kadhi khichri*. Don't be fooled by the humble ingredients, or by the fact that in Gujarati households it's the simplest everyday fare; it's wonderfully subtle and soothing. *Kadhi khichri* is a beautiful partnership: delicately perfumed golden rice with split mung (*khichri*) served with sour, gently spiced buttermilk (*kadhi*) poured over the rice. *Kadhi khichri* makes a lovely light meal in itself, but a sublime addition would be Aubergine and Potato Curry (page 28). In fact, *khichri* can be served with any 'wet' vegetable curry (the combination of rice and beans would contribute protein to the meal, too), but do try it with *kadhi*. I'm sure you'll see why it is such a classic.

1 cup basmati rice

½ cup *moong dal* (yellow split mung beans)

50g/2oz/¼ cup butter

7.5cm/3in cinnamon stick

4 cardamoms

3 cloves

8–10 peppercorns

½ teaspoon cumin seeds

1 small onion, finely chopped

1 clove garlic, finely chopped

2 green chillies, sliced

10 or so curry leaves

½ teaspoon turmeric

1 teaspoon salt

TO SERVE

Kadhi (page 76; make it while the rice is cooking – see notes in the method)

Serves 4

Wash the rice and *dal* and soak in warm water for 20 minutes (put a timer on – soaking the rice for too long makes it difficult to achieve fluffy, separate grains at the end of cooking).

Melt the butter in a deep, medium-sized pan over a low heat. When it foams, add the cinnamon, cardamoms, cloves, peppercorns and cumin seeds. After a minute or so, when their fragrance is rising, add the onion, garlic, chillies and curry leaves. Cook gently until the onion is translucent – about 5 minutes.

Add the turmeric, cook for a minute or so further, then add 2½ cups of hot water and the salt and increase the heat to high. Once the water begins to bubble, sprinkle in the drained rice and *dal*. Return to the boil, then turn the heat right down, so that the water is just faintly bubbling. Put on a lid and cook as gently as you can (do not stir from now on) until all the liquid has been absorbed. This should take about 25 minutes. (While the *khichri* is cooking, make the *kadhi* as instructed on page 76.) Check the *khichri* periodically: to see if the water has been absorbed without disturbing the rice too much, take a knife and part the rice from the side of the pan to peek down to the bottom. If the water is gone, but rice and *dal* are not yet cooked, add a little more boiling water. As soon as the rice is cooked, cover the pan with a tea towel or double thickness of kitchen paper, then the lid. This will help to keep the rice grains separate until you're ready to serve.

Spiced buttermilk
Kadhi

This non-rice dish is included here as it is the classic accompaniment to the preceding recipe – it seemed madness to put it anywhere else in the book. Classically partnered with *Chuthi Khichri* (page 74), *kadhi* can also be served in a bowl or cup, like a drink, with any Indian meal.

....

2 cloves garlic

2cm/1in ginger

2 green chillies

1 teaspoon salt

1 teaspoon cumin seeds

325ml/12fl oz yoghurt

2 teaspoons *besan* (gram or chickpea flour)

1/8 teaspoon turmeric

1 teaspoon brown sugar

2 branches of curry leaves

1 tablespoon sunflower oil

1 dried red Kashmiri chilli

1/2 teaspoon mustard seeds

Pinch of fenugreek seeds

4 cloves

1/4 teaspoon asafoetida

2 tablespoons chopped coriander (cilantro) leaves

IF YOU ARE MAKING THIS to eat with *chuthi khichri*, and one dish is ready before the other, don't worry. The rice will stay warm off the heat with its lid on for quite a while, or the *kadhi* can be kept hot over very low heat until the *khichri* is ready.

Makes 300ml/10fl oz – enough for 4 with *Chuthi Khichri* (page 74)

....

Crush together the garlic, ginger, chillie salt and 1/2 teaspoon of the cumin seeds and set aside. Put the yoghurt in the goblet of a blender – or use a jug (pitcher) and hand-held blender as I do – and add 750ml/1 1/4 pints/3 cups of water. Blend thoroughly. Pour off all but about a quarter of this mixture into another container and reserve. Add the *besan* to the remaining mixture in the blender goblet and blend thoroughly again. Now pour the reserved yoghurt and water mixture back into the blender with the turmeric, brown sugar and the garlic-ginger paste, and blend again. Add the curry leaves and set aside.

Heat the oil in a small pan over medium heat. Break the dried red chilli into two and add it to the pan – don't get your face anywhere near the pan as the fumes from the chilli will make your eyes smart. Wait for a few seconds while the chilli darkens, then – just as it turns black – add the mustard seeds, the remaining 1/2 teaspoon cumin seeds, the fenugreek seeds and cloves. After 20 seconds add the asafoetida. Let the spices cook very briefly before adding the yoghurt mixture, stirring constantly but gently until it boils. Add half the coriander leaves and cook very gently for 10 minutes, stirring often to keep it from sticking. Add the remaining coriander, then serve spooned over the rice, or in a cup or bowl.

Creamy rice and mung beans
Naram khichri

When I first found out about this dish it took me completely by surprise – I had never thought such a thing would exist in Indian cooking: absolutely unspiced rice and beans, cooked down to the creamy consistency of risotto (*khichri* is often translated as 'porridge', but I don't think this makes it sound as tempting as it really is). I don't want you to be put off when I tell you that in our house we call it 'grey' *khichri*, a nickname my wife Salima gave the dish as a child because of the pale olive green colour the rice turns as it cooks with the mung beans. Let me reassure you: it is not at all unappetising to look at, and it tastes wonderful. In her childhood, 'grey' *khichri* was pure comfort to Salima: on cold, grey winter days, it warmed her up as no other dish could.

Naram khichri makes a comforting and absorbent accompaniment to 'wet' curries – that is, anything richly flavoured with a good amount of sauce, for instance Lamb Curry (page 56), Fish Curry (page 44) or Masala-stuffed Aubergines (page 24). It's a good alternative to plain boiled rice and is hardly any more work: though it does take a little more time to cook, it pretty much looks after itself.

Butter is used to enrich this frugal dish, and you can be as moderate or extravagant as you wish – my quantities are simply a guideline.

....

1 cup basmati rice

¾ cup split green mung beans (the type with the green husk left on)

1½ teaspoons salt

25g/1oz/2 tablespoons butter

Enough for 4 as a side dish

....

Wash the rice and mung beans together in warm water. Put them in a deep, medium-sized pan with 6 cups of cold water. Set the pan on the heat with the lid off (this is important – with the lid on, the pan will boil over, making a starchy mess all over the stove). Bring to the boil, skimming off scum as it appears. To achieve the correct texture, it's important that you do not stir the cooking rice and beans.

Once boiling, reduce the heat to maintain the faintest simmer and put the lid on, but leave a gap for the steam to escape. After about 20 minutes, the rice will be cooked and the beans tender, but both maintaining their shape. There should still be some water in the pan (to check, take a spatula and pull the mixture away from the side of the pan to peek at the bottom). If there is no water left in the pan, add a cup of boiling water. At this stage, sprinkle in the salt.

Cook until the rice is breaking down and the beans are squashy (this can take anywhere between 10 and 20 minutes). Make sure the mixture does not get dry – the finished *khichri* should have the consistency of risotto or thick porridge – add boiling water as required. Once it begins to look slightly curdled – as the starch escapes from the rice grains into the water – turn off the heat. Drop in the butter and put the lid back on for a minute or so. Once the butter melts, beat with a wooden spoon until creamy. Check the seasoning, add more butter if you wish, then serve immediately.

Peas pilau
Mattar pilau

This aromatic dish, combining sweet-scented rice, peas, potatoes and eggs, must be one of the best-loved recipes in this book. Its universal appeal is down to the fact that it is, I think, a perfect combination of simplicity and subtle refinement. We often have it for a weekday lunch, and yet have served it with great success at family gatherings (at which times Rose makes a batch so huge, the giant pot straddles the whole stove and she has to stand on a chair to stir it). Avowed carnivores (like the Hiranis) will eat it without complaint – its spicing is, unusually, similar to meat dishes, and the eggs help make it feel very satisfying. And it's happily adapted for kids – just leave out the chillies (but remember to remove the whole spices before serving to small children). We weaned our son Haroun on a chilli-free version and he still makes special requests for *Peas-pea*, as he calls it.

On a restaurant menu, this dish would most probably be offered as an accompaniment to curries. But actually it is usually served as the main event – as a vegetarian main course, much as *Akhni* (pages 82–84) would be served to meat eaters. In fact, when my wife stopped eating meat years ago, Rose cooked this for her instead of *akhni*, which had been a Sunday night fixture since childhood. Peas pilau is always served with the chunky tomato and cucumber salad *Kachumber* (page 138). Once you've tried peas pilau, I think the combination of textures and Rose's subtle spicing will make this dish a regular fixture in your house too.

Serves 4

2 cups basmati rice

5 cloves garlic

3.5cm/1½in ginger

2½ teaspoons salt

1½ teaspoons cumin seeds

10cm/4in cinnamon stick, broken into 2 pieces

6 cardamoms

4 cloves

8 peppercorns

3 tablespoons groundnut (peanut) oil

1 large onion, quartered and thinly sliced

4 green chillies, thickly sliced

4 small potatoes, peeled and cut into 5cm/2in dice

2 tomatoes, finely chopped, or 135ml/5fl oz crushed canned plum tomatoes and juice (about a third of a can)

½ teaspoon turmeric

225g/8oz/1 cup frozen peas

4 eggs, boiled for 6 minutes and shelled

Wash the rice in several changes of water, then soak in warm water for 20 minutes. Pound the garlic, ginger and salt to a paste and set aside. Put the cumin seeds, broken cinnamon stick, cardamom pods, cloves and peppercorns in a glass filled with water and soak for 5 minutes.

Heat the oil in a large pan and fry the onion over medium heat, stirring frequently, until it begins to turn golden-brown. Add the chillies and stir well. Cook for a minute or so, then drain the soaking spices and add them to the onion. Cook for a few minutes and, when aromatic, add the garlic-ginger paste. Stir well,   »

» reduce the heat and cook gently for 1 minute. Add the potatoes, tomatoes and turmeric and bring up to simmering point. Cook the *masala* over medium heat until the oil pools around the sides of the pan. Add 3 cups of water and the frozen peas, and bring to the boil.

Drain and add the rice, stir and bring back up to simmering point. Cover and cook for 5 minutes before reducing the heat to low to cook the rice slowly, for about 15 minutes, without stirring. Then gently tuck the eggs into the rice and continue cooking with the lid on until the rice is just cooked. Don't stir the rice yet, but watch the water level – take a spoon and gently part a little of the rice from the side of the pan to allow you

to peek down at the bottom. If the water has been absorbed before the rice is cooked, add more boiling water (say half a cupful at a time) and continue cooking and checking the water until the rice is just cooked.

Turn off the heat, lift the lid and put a clean tea towel across the top of the pan to absorb steam and help prevent the rice turning soggy. Clap on the lid again and allow the pilau to stand for just a few minutes before serving.

SERVE A SPECIAL KACHUMBER, made with one or two extra chillies, for chilli-loving adults to compensate for the lack of heat in a child-friendly batch of peas pilau.

Lamb pilau
Ghosh ni akhni

Within her community, Rose is justly famous for several dishes, amongst them *akhni* (she has been told that no one makes it like her). This delicious marriage of meat and rice is often served at social gatherings, so I've had a chance to sample a few versions and I have to agree: I've never had better *akhni* than Rose's.

Take a glance down the ingredients list and you might think there's little difference between *akhni* and *biriani* – but in that assumption you'd be entirely wrong. What distinguishes them is down to the cooking and final presentation: whereas *biriani* is essentially a rich sauce thickened with fried onions and served on a bed of scented, saffron-tinted rice, *akhni* is gentler, subtler and altogether different. Rice, meat, onions, spices and potatoes are combined and gently cooked – casseroled, almost – to produce a delicately flavoured result. This version with lamb was a favourite of Rose's mother, Rhemat, and a regular Sunday-night treat in my wife's childhood (she tells me that when she was young she would rather eat *akhni* than any other dish). If *biriani* is the perfect celebratory dish, then *akhni* is the dish for an understated dinner with good friends you don't need to impress, but really want to spoil.

Traditionally *akhni* would be served with *Samosa* (pages 163–67) alongside and perhaps a vegetable curry, but more often than not we serve this simply with *Kachumber* (page 138) or *Sambharo* (page 138) – you can accompany it with any pickle from the book.

FOR THE MARINADE

2 fat cloves garlic

2cm/1in ginger

½ teaspoon cumin seeds

½ teaspoon salt

1 tablespoon yoghurt

450g/1lb lamb from the shoulder or leg, cut into 5cm/2in chunks with bone retained, trimmed of fat and rinsed to remove stray splinters of bone

FOR THE RICE

4 cloves garlic

4cm/1½in ginger

4 green chillies

2 teaspoons salt

2 cups basmati rice

2.5cm/1in cinnamon stick

5 cardamoms

6 cloves

12 peppercorns

2 teaspoons cumin seeds

2 tablespoons groundnut (peanut) oil

10g/½oz/1 tablespoon butter

1 medium onion, halved and sliced into half-moons from root to tip

4 tomatoes, skinned and finely chopped

4 medium-sized potatoes, peeled and cut into 7cm/3in chunks

Serves 4

To make the marinade, pound the garlic, ginger, cumin seeds and salt to a paste using a pestle and mortar. Add the yoghurt and mix thoroughly.

Put the meat in a medium-sized pan, then add the yoghurt marinade and mix thoroughly. Set aside for 20 minutes in the fridge, then place over high heat and bring to the boil. Boil rapidly for 10 minutes with the lid on. Add 750ml/1¼ pints/3 cups of boiling water and reduce the heat to a simmer. Cook until the meat is quite tender, for approximately 1 hour.

While you wait for the meat to cook, start preparing the rice. Pound the garlic, ginger, green chillies and 1 teaspoon of the salt to a paste. Set aside.

When the meat has been cooking for 40 minutes, wash the rice in several changes of water, until the water runs clear. Soak the rice in warm water for 20 minutes while you make the *masala*.

Put the cinnamon, cardamoms, cloves, peppercorns and cumin seeds in a glass of water. Stand for a few minutes while you heat the oil and butter in a large pan. Drain the whole spices in a sieve and add to the pan; they will sizzle and release their scent. Add the onion and fry over medium heat, stirring constantly, until the onion is golden-brown.

Add the garlic-ginger paste, fry for a few seconds, then add the chopped tomatoes and the potatoes.

Increase the heat to high and cook the *masala* rapidly until the tomatoes break down and the oil pools around the sides of the pan. Lift the cooked meat from its cooking liquor (but reserve the liquid), add it to the *masala* and simmer for 5 more minutes to combine the flavours.

Pour the reserved meat cooking liquor into a jug (pitcher) and add enough hot water to make 3 cups of liquid. Add it to the *masala* with the last teaspoon of salt and bring to the boil.

Drain the rice and add it to the pan. Stir thoroughly but gently, then return to the boil. Put the lid on the pan and cook the rice rapidly for 10 minutes, then reduce the heat and simmer very gently until the rice is almost cooked – it should retain just a little bite. (You may need to turn the rice from time to time: you should do this gently and deftly, aiming to break the cooking rice as little as possible.) Check if you need to add more water by taking a wooden spoon and gently parting a little of the rice from the side of the pan so you can peek down to the bottom. If the water is gone before the rice is cooked, add a little boiling water.

When almost done, turn off the rice, top the pan with a double thickness of kitchen paper and cover with the lid. Leave it to stand, so that the rice can finish cooking in the residual heat.

Chicken pilau
Kukra ni akhni

More than a mere variation on the traditional lamb *akhni*, this recipe has a slightly different balance of flavours to make the best of chicken's delicacy. It's a lovely meal in its own right; the usual accompaniments – *Kachumber* (page 138), *Raitha* (page 130) and Lemon Salt Pickle (page 126) – all work well.

1.8kg/4lb chicken, jointed and skinned (or use the same weight of chicken pieces)
4 cloves garlic
7.5cm/3in ginger
6 green chillies, trimmed and halved
2 teaspoons salt
2 tablespoons yoghurt
3 cups basmati rice
50g/2oz/$\frac{1}{4}$ cup butter (or 3 tablespoons oil)
2 medium onions, halved and sliced into half-moons from root to tip
7.5cm/3in cinnamon stick
5 cardamoms
4 cloves
12 peppercorns
3 teaspoons cumin seeds
6 medium potatoes, peeled and halved
4 tomatoes, finely chopped

Serves 6

First deal with the chicken pieces. Chop the breasts into 4 and thighs into 2 using a heavy knife or, preferably, a meat cleaver if you have one. Rinse the meat thoroughly to remove any stray splinters of bone, then drain and pat the pieces dry with kitchen paper.

Pound the garlic, ginger, chillies and salt to a paste. Mix with the yoghurt, then put the chicken and the yoghurt mixture into a non-reactive bowl. Cover and refrigerate for 1 hour. After an hour has passed, wash the basmati rice well in several changes of cold water until the water is clear. Set to soak in warm water for 20 minutes while you prepare the *masala*.

Melt the butter (or heat the oil) in a large, deep pan. Add the onions and cook over medium heat until they turn pale gold. Meanwhile, put the cinnamon, cardamoms, cloves, peppercorns and cumin seeds into a glass of water and soak for 1 minute, then drain and add to the onions.

Cook for 2 minutes more, then, when the spices are fragrant, add the potatoes and the chicken with its marinade. Stir well and increase the heat to high. Bring to the boil and simmer rapidly for 10 minutes, then add the tomatoes.

Simmer for 5 more minutes, then add 4 cups of water. Bring up to the boil, then add the drained rice. Stir well and ensure that everything is submerged as you bring it back up to the boil. Cook at a brisk simmer for 5 minutes, then reduce the heat to its lowest setting, cover and cook gently until the chicken and rice are cooked and the liquid is absorbed. You may need to add a little more water to reach this stage – use a wooden spoon to part a little of the rice from the side of the pan so you can peek at the bottom. If it gets dry before the chicken and rice are cooked, add boiling water, a little at a time, until everything's done.

Lamb biriani
Ghosh biriani

Moghul in origin, hailing from north India, this grand feast dish is now made throughout the subcontinent in a variety of ways. This excellent version is from Rose's sister-in-law Mariam, from her native Madras. Marinate the meat the night before for best results, and serve the biriani with *Kachumber* (page 138) and *Raitha* (page 130).

700g/1½lb lamb from the shoulder or leg, cut into large chunks with bone retained, trimmed of fat and rinsed to remove stray splinters of bone

125ml/4fl oz/½ cup yoghurt

1 bay leaf, broken in half

1 quantity Spiced Roast Potatoes (page 89)*

1 quantity Biriani Rice (page 89)*

4 tablespoons groundnut (peanut) oil

5 large onions, quartered and thinly sliced

4 fat cloves garlic

5cm/2in ginger

3 green chillies

1 teaspoon salt

1 teaspoon *dhana jiru* (page 16)

½ teaspoon chilli powder

¼ teaspoon turmeric

400g/14oz can plum tomatoes and juice, crushed

½ tablespoon finely chopped coriander (cilantro) stems

1 tablespoon chopped coriander (cilantro) leaves

½ teaspoon *garam masala* (page 16)

2 tablespoons melted butter

* These items can be prepared while you cook the lamb; see notes in the method.

Serves 4

Combine the lamb, yoghurt and one half of the bay leaf in a small, non-reactive pan. Cover and leave overnight in the fridge. When you're ready to cook, set the pan on the hob over high heat. Boil rapidly for 10 minutes, then reduce the heat and simmer gently until the meat is soft – this will take 40 minutes to an hour. Add hot water as necessary, to stop the mixture becoming dry. Meanwhile, roast the potatoes and cook the rice.

Set the cooked meat aside. Warm the oil in a large pan and fry the onions over medium heat until golden-brown, stirring frequently. Remove 3 tablespoons of them and set aside. Pound the garlic, ginger, chillies and salt to a paste and add to the onions in the pan with the *dhana jiru*, chilli powder and turmeric. Stir well, then add the tomatoes and the remaining half bay leaf. Bring to a simmer and cook until the oil pools around the sides of the pan. Add the meat and juices and the coriander stems and simmer for 10 minutes. Fold in the roast potatoes, *garam masala* and coriander leaves. Turn off the heat.

Now assemble the biriani. In a large heavy-based pan arrange a layer of a third of the rice. Drizzle over 1 tablespoon of melted butter. Cover with 1 tablespoon of the reserved fried onions and half the meat sauce. Top with a layer of half the remaining rice and repeat the process, finishing with the last portion of rice. Trickle 1 tablespoon of water down the sides of the pan, cover and cook gently for 10 minutes. Serve on a platter, scattered with the remaining fried onions.

Chicken biriani
Kukra ni biriani

This dish is entirely different from lamb biriani –
more akin to *Kalyo* (page 60) in its blend of
yoghurt, saffron and spices. True to its origins as
a Moghul feast dish, it takes time to prepare, but
is rewardingly aromatic and refined. Serve with
Kachumber (page 138) and *Raitha* (page 130).

1 small chicken, about 1.2kg/3lb in weight,
jointed (or the same weight of chicken pieces),
skinned and breasts halved

8 cloves garlic

7.5cm/3in ginger

2 teaspoons salt

5cm/2in cinnamon stick

3 cardamoms

4 cloves

10 peppercorns

2 tablespoons yoghurt

1 teaspoon chilli powder

$\frac{1}{8}$ teaspoon turmeric

400g/14oz can plum tomatoes and
juice, crushed

1 quantity Spiced Roast Potatoes (see page 89) *

110g/4oz ready-fried onions (or 6 large onions,
prepared as described on page 19) *

1 quantity Biriani Rice (see page 89) *

Large pinch of saffron strands

30g/1oz/2 tablespoons butter

$\frac{1}{2}$ teaspoon *garam masala* (page 16)

2 teaspoons lemon juice, or to taste

1 tablespoon chopped coriander
(cilantro) leaves

** These items can be prepared while marinating
and cooking the chicken; see notes in the method.*

For 4 people

Put the chicken pieces in a large saucepan.
Crush the garlic and ginger with the salt,
then add it to the chicken with the cinnamon
stick, cardamoms, cloves, peppercorns, yoghurt,
chilli powder, turmeric and tomatoes. Mix
thoroughly, then cover the pan and set it aside
in the fridge for an hour. In the meantime, you
can prepare the roast potatoes and fried onions
(if you are using fresh ones).

When the chicken has marinated for an hour,
set the pan on the heat and bring to the boil.
Cook rapidly for 15 minutes, then reduce the
heat and simmer gently for around half an hour
or until the meat is tender and cooked through.
Meanwhile, cook the rice and pop it into a low
oven (150°C/300°F/gas mark 2) with the roast
potatoes to keep them warm until you're ready
to assemble the dish. In a small bowl, steep the
saffron strands in a tablespoon of warm water.

Reserve 2 tablespoons of fried onions for garnish
and add the remainder to the chicken with the
butter, *garam masala* and lemon juice and stir
well. Cook for 5 more minutes, then turn off the
heat. Add the roast potatoes just before you are
ready to eat (so that they don't turn soggy),
stirring them well to coat with *masala*.

To serve, arrange a bed of the rice on a large
platter. Sprinkle with the saffron strands and
water, then mound the chicken in the centre on
top of the rice. Sprinkle with the reserved fried
onions and scatter with the coriander leaves.

Whole lentil biriani
Masoor biriani

This combination of richly savoury *masala*, tender lentils and light, fragrant rice will appeal to meat eaters and vegetarians alike. Serve with *Kachumber* (page 138) and *Raitha* (page 130) for a special (yet inexpensive) meal with friends.

1½ cups whole brown lentils (*masoor*), rinsed

1 quantity Spiced Roast Potatoes (see opposite)*

4 cloves garlic

4cm/1½in ginger

1½ teaspoons salt

4 tablespoons groundnut (peanut) oil

4 large onions, quartered and thinly sliced

25g/1oz/2 tablespoons butter

400g/14oz can plum tomatoes and juice, crushed

½ teaspoon *dhana jiru* (page 16)

1 teaspoon chilli powder

¼ teaspoon turmeric

½ tablespoon chopped coriander (cilantro) stems

1 quantity Biriani Rice (see opposite)*

Large pinch of saffron strands

Garam masala (page 16) for sprinkling

2 tablespoons chopped coriander (cilantro) leaves

Sliced green chillies to garnish (optional)

* These items can be prepared while cooking the lentils; see notes in the method.

Serves 4

Put the lentils in a small pan with 3 cups of water. Boil rapidly for 10 minutes, then reduce the heat and simmer for about 20 minutes more, until the lentils are soft but retaining their shape. While they cook, roast the potatoes – and leave the oven on for later. Pound the garlic, ginger and salt to a paste and set aside.

Heat the oil in a pan and fry the onions over medium heat, stirring constantly until golden-brown. Remove half of the onions and set aside. Reduce the heat to low and add the butter to the remaining onions in the pan. When melted, add the garlic-ginger paste, cook for 30 seconds, then add the tomatoes, *dhana jiru*, chilli powder, turmeric and coriander stems. Bring up to simmering point and cook until the oil pools around the sides of the pan. While it simmers, cook the rice. In a small bowl, steep the saffron strands in a tablespoon of warm water.

Drain the lentils, add them to the *masala* and cook for 10 minutes or so to combine the flavours. Add the potatoes and set aside.

In a wide ovenproof dish make a layer of a third of the rice. Sprinkle with a teaspoon of the saffron strands and water, a third of the reserved fried onions, a large pinch of *garam masala*, and a teaspoon of the coriander. Cover with a third of the lentil mixture (try to ensure the potatoes are evenly distributed). Repeat with 2 more layers of rice (sprinkling saffron, onions, *garam masala* and coriander as you go) and lentils.

Trickle 2 tablespoons of water down the sides of the dish, then cover. Put in the oven, reduce the temperature to 140°C/285°F/gas mark 1 and cook for 30 minutes. Serve on a platter scattered with the remaining coriander and the chillies.

Biriani rice
Biriani chawal

The preparation of the rice element is the same for all types of biriani. It's important not to overcook the rice as, in most cases, it will be reheated with the sauce, so take care.

2 cups basmati rice

1 teaspoon salt

4cm/1½in cinnamon stick

2 cardamoms

3 cloves

10 peppercorns

For dishes serving 4 people

Wash the rice well and drain, then put it in a large pan with plenty of cold water, the salt, cinnamon stick, cardamoms, cloves and peppercorns, and bring to the boil. Cook for 7–10 minutes, until just tender but still retaining a little bite. Drain thoroughly, remove the whole spices and cover the pan with a clean tea towel – this will help the rice stay fluffy until you're ready to assemble the biriani.

Spiced roast potatoes
Sekela bateta

Many rice dishes (and some others, too) include these potatoes; I guess they were originally added to stretch quantities to feed more people, but they're a delicious addition even if you're not feeding unexpected extra guests! Roasting is healthier than traditional deep-frying, and allows you to get on with preparing the rest of the meal; in the oven the potatoes can be cooked in a tiny amount of oil and look after themselves.

4 medium potatoes, peeled and halved

½ tablespoon groundnut (peanut) oil

1 clove garlic, crushed

Large pinch of salt

Large pinch of chilli powder

⅛ teaspoon turmeric

For dishes serving 4 people

Preheat the oven to 220°C/425°F/gas mark 7. In an ovenproof dish, toss the potatoes with the oil, garlic, salt, chilli powder and turmeric. Put the dish in the oven and roast the potatoes for 25 minutes until they are golden-brown and cooked through – test them by piercing with a skewer or the point of a knife.

THESE POTATOES are also excellent just as they are as a side dish – try them with Spiced Roast Lamb (page 58), for instance.

Beans and lentils

To Rose's distant ancestors, farming families scratching a living in the dusty desert plains of Gujarat, pulses must have been a godsend. Unperishables packed with protein, dried peas and beans – *dal* as they're known in India (usually indicating an unhusked, split pulse) – would have been a crucial staple for leaner times. Today, even in times of plenty, you'll still find beans and lentils on the menu. *Dal* unites all classes, castes and religions, and is served across the subcontinent at any time of day. Eaten mixed with rice or sipped from a cup or bowl, *dal* can be thick and spoonable, or soupy and light. There's a wide variety of pulses to choose from and myriad ways to cook them; we cover a small but varied selection here. All of our recipes are fairly quick to cook – lentils need little or no soaking before cooking. Although Rose often uses dried beans, soaking them overnight and cooking them for a couple of hours, we've opted for the convenience of canned beans in our recipes. For me, this transforms these traditionally slow-simmered dishes into brilliant standbys for the end of a busy working day, or a late-night post-pub supper rustled up in just fifteen minutes.

STORE YOUR PULSES in airtight containers away from bright light and they will keep for long periods of time. But unless you plan to eat *dal* daily, don't be tempted to bulk-buy dried beans and lentils. Although they can keep for years, over time their flavour will deteriorate, and they will take longer to cook as they get older. Instead, buy smallish quantities of a few different pulses and use them up quickly.

Basic dal
Daar

Dal in a very similar form to this recipe – a soupy mixture of lentils enhanced with herbs and spices – is the most basic, inexpensive and ubiquitous of foods in India. But even this, the lowest common denominator of Indian food, does not escape Rose's refining touches; delicate accents of mustard, coriander (cilantro) and lemon bring subtle depth and savour. Served with just plain boiled basmati rice, salad leaves and some Lemon Salt Pickle (page 126) – the perfect accompaniment – it makes a lovely, light and frugal meal, but it also works well served with a selection of different curries.

....

175g/6oz/scant cup *moong dal* (yellow split mung beans without the skin)

50g/2oz/4 tablespoons *masoor dal* (red split lentils)

4 green chillies

1 fat clove garlic

2.5cm/1in ginger, peeled

1½ teaspoons salt

2 tomatoes, skinned and chopped

1 tablespoon groundnut (peanut) oil

½ teaspoon mustard seeds

1 small onion, finely chopped

½ tablespoon butter

½ teaspoon *dhana jiru* (page 16)

¼ teaspoon turmeric

½ tablespoon finely chopped coriander (cilantro) stems

Lemon juice to taste (optional)

½ tablespoon roughly chopped coriander (cilantro) leaves

Serves 4 with rice, or more as part of a larger meal

....

Wash both *dal* in several changes of water until the water is clear. Drain and put them in a pot with 2 litres/3½ pints/8 cups of water. Bring to the boil without the lid. Skim off any scum that rises to the surface of the water. Reduce the heat to a simmer and cook the *dal* for 20 minutes or until it is soft and has broken down completely.

While the *dal* cooks, make the *masala*. Top and tail 2 of the green chillies, cut into short lengths and use a pestle and mortar to crush them with the garlic, ginger and salt. Add the tomatoes and pound the mixture to combine.

Heat the oil in a separate pan, add the mustard seeds and onion and fry until pale gold. Add the butter and, when melted, add the *dhana jiru* and turmeric. Cook the spices for a few seconds, then add the tomato mixture and the coriander stems. Increase the heat and simmer the *masala* until the tomatoes break down and the oil pools around the sides of the pan. Set aside.

When the *dal* is cooked, take a whisk and beat the mixture to make it as smooth as possible. Then add it to the cooked *masala* with the remaining 2 chillies (left whole). Bring the mixture to the boil and simmer for 10 minutes. Add more water if necessary – it should have the consistency of thin soup.

Taste the mixture, adding more salt and some lemon juice to sharpen the flavour as you like. Scatter over the coriander leaves and serve.

Whole black lentils with chilli
Urad nu saak

Hailing from the Punjab, this sturdy, satisfying stew is perfect nourishment for a race of warriors (as the Punjabis are known in their homeland).

Rose was given this recipe by a Punjabi work colleague who had a generous hand with the *ghee* – and though the dish was utterly delicious, Rose decided to adapt the recipe to use just a little butter and some oil for a healthy but still delicious result. If you were served this dish in the Punjab, it would be garnished with fine shreds of ginger, but Rose prefers to serve her version ungarnished.

Serve this dish with *Varela Parotha* (page 118), *Naan* (page 114) or Chappatis (page 108), for a simple, nutritious meal, or offer it with a selection of curries.

....

225g/8oz/1 cup *urad* (whole black lentils), rinsed

3 tablespoons olive oil

25g/1oz/2 tablespoons butter

2 medium onions, chopped

4 cloves garlic, finely chopped

3 green chillies, finely chopped

$\frac{1}{2}$ teaspoon turmeric

6 tablespoons crushed canned plum tomatoes and juice

1 teaspoon salt

$\frac{1}{2}$ tablespoon finely chopped coriander (cilantro) leaves

$\frac{1}{2}$ tablespoon finely shredded ginger to garnish (optional)

Serves 4 with bread, or more as part of a larger meal

....

Put the *urad* and 1 litre/1$\frac{3}{4}$ pints/4 cups of water into a pan and bring to the boil. Simmer rapidly for 10 minutes, then reduce the heat and simmer gently for about 35 minutes until the lentils are quite soft and split. As they cook, add boiling water as necessary to keep the lentils well covered. When the lentils are done, turn off the heat and set aside.

Heat the oil and butter in a medium pan and add the onions. Cook gently until they are just translucent, but not browned, then add the garlic, chilli and turmeric. Cook for a minute only, then add the tomatoes and salt. Bring everything up to a simmer and cook until the oil pools around the sides of the pan.

Add the cooked *urad* and its water and simmer for 10 minutes more to combine the flavours. Taste for salt, adjusting if necessary, and sprinkle with the chopped coriander and ginger (if using). Serve hot.

Split chickpeas and bottle gourd
Dudhi ane channa daar

When Rose was 15, she lived in an apartment building in Kampala, Uganda, populated with other Indian families. One day, she was playing hide and seek with her friends and had just found a good place to hide on the third floor when she became aware of a wonderful smell. Something delicious was cooking nearby and, enticed by the scent, she abandoned her hiding place to investigate. She followed her nose to the apartment where a huge pot of *dal* and vegetables was cooking. The kind lady cook gave Rose a little of the *dal* to take home; the next day Rose was back asking to be shown how the dish was prepared – after many years of cooking and refining, this recipe is the result.

Bottle gourd, or *dudhi*, can be found in Indian and Asian supermarkets. It looks rather like a long, straight-sided green aubergine (eggplant) – see the picture on page 23. Buy a small one that feels hard and heavy for its size. If you can't find *dudhi*, aubergine, or courgettes (zucchini) make suitable substitutes.

350g/12oz/1½ cups *channa dal* (split chickpeas)

6 cloves garlic

1cm/½in ginger

2 teaspoons salt

2 tablespoons groundnut (peanut) oil

1 medium onion, chopped

2 green chillies, chopped

1½ teaspoons *dhana jiru* (page 16)

½ teaspoon turmeric

300ml/10fl oz crushed canned plum tomatoes and juice (about three-quarters of a can)

½ tablespoon chopped coriander (cilantro) leaves, plus extra to serve

1 small bottle gourd (*dudhi*), about 225g/8oz in weight, peeled and cut into 2.5cm/1in pieces

1 teaspoon lemon juice, or more to taste

Enough for 4 with rice

Wash the *dal*, picking out and discarding any shrivelled or dark pieces. Put in a pot with 1 litre/1¾ pints/4 cups of cold water and bring up to simmering point. Simmer gently until the lentils are tender, but retaining their shape (this should take 20–30 minutes). Add more water as necessary to prevent the lentils boiling dry.

While the *dal* is cooking, make the *masala*. Pound the garlic, ginger and 1 teaspoon of the salt to a paste. Heat the oil in a medium pan and fry the onion gently until golden-brown. Add the garlic-ginger paste and the chopped chillies and cook for a few seconds before adding the *dhana jiru*, turmeric, tomatoes, coriander and the remaining teaspoon of salt. Stir well to combine.

Add the bottle gourd cubes, stir well and cover. Simmer gently for about 15–20 minutes until the bottle gourd is tender. When the *dal* is cooked, stir it and its cooking liquid into the bottle gourd mixture. Warm the mixture through, taking care not to overcook the *dal* or the bottle gourd. Add the lemon juice to sharpen up the flavour, then taste and add more if you like. Sprinkle with coriander leaves and serve with boiled basmati rice and sliced onions.

Mung beans with yoghurt
Mug nu saak

This wonderful dish is one of the first recipes I learned from Rose. At the time, my wife and I were living in Hong Kong and Rose came to visit; Salima had been missing her mum's cooking and, as chief cook, I was ordered to learn a few key recipes. It's testament to the wonderful flavour of this simple dish that it was selected as an essential recipe for me to learn.

For most of his life, Rose's husband refused to eat this dish with yoghurt – he had never tried it, but for some reason he was suspicious of it. But one day Rose forgot to separate his portion before stirring in the yoghurt, so he was forced to eat it – upon which he declared (roughly translated from the Gujarati), "Why have I never tried this before? It's fantastic!"

175g/6oz/¾ cup whole mung beans, rinsed

2 tablespoons groundnut (peanut) oil

½ teaspoon mustard seeds

½ teaspoon cumin seeds

Large pinch of asafoetida

200ml/7fl oz crushed canned plum tomatoes and juice (about half a can)

2 green chillies

2 cloves garlic, crushed with 1 teaspoon salt

½ tablespoon finely chopped coriander (cilantro) stems

2 teaspoons *dhana jiru* (page 16)

½–1 teaspoon chilli powder (to taste)

½ teaspoon turmeric

6 tablespoons yoghurt

Lemon juice, to taste

1 tablespoon chopped coriander (cilantro) leaves

Serves 4 with plain boiled rice

Put the mung beans in a deep pot with 1.2 litres/2 pints/4 cups of cold water. Bring to the boil, then reduce the heat and simmer for around 45 minutes until the beans are soft and beginning to split open – but stop cooking before they turn to complete mush.

In the meantime, prepare the *masala*. Put the oil in a medium-sized pan and heat gently. Add the mustard and cumin seeds and cook until they begin to sizzle. Add the asafoetida, cook for a few seconds, then stir in the tomatoes.

Cut the green chillies in half along their length and prick the skins with the tip of the knife. Add to the tomatoes in the pan. Then add the garlic paste, coriander stems, *dhana jiru*, chilli powder and turmeric. Increase the heat so that the sauce simmers rapidly, stirring frequently, until the oil pools around the sides of the pan.

Once the mung beans are cooked, tip them and their cooking water into the simmering *masala*. Bring to the boil, then simmer gently for 10 minutes to allow the flavours to combine.

Combine the yoghurt with 275ml/½ pint/1 cup of water. Stir this mixture into the beans. Cook gently for a couple of minutes until the yoghurt is heated through, then check the seasoning – add salt if necessary (you may need more than you expect) and some lemon juice to taste (this dish should have a slightly sharp flavour). Throw over the chopped coriander leaves and serve.

Moong dal with spinach
Bhaji vari mug ni daar

I love this simple, tasty combination of *dal* and lightly cooked spinach. It's a perfect side dish to many of the meat dishes, served with any of the breads in this book, especially Millet Flatbread (page 117) or Flaky Flatbreads (page 118). If you're buying spinach from a greengrocer in bunches, look for a variety with a pinkish tinge at the base of the stems – this has a good flavour and is less acidic than other kinds.

....

225g/8oz/1 cup *moong dal* (hulled, split mung beans)

2 tablespoons groundnut (peanut) oil

2 fat cloves garlic, finely chopped

2 green chillies, finely chopped

$\frac{1}{2}$ teaspoon *dhana jiru* (page 16)

$\frac{1}{4}$ teaspoon turmeric

200ml/7fl oz crushed canned plum tomatoes and juice (about half a can)

1 teaspoon salt

3 bunches of spinach (or 2 x 180g/6oz packs), washed thoroughly to remove grit, coarse stems discarded

Serves 2 generously with bread, or 6 as part of a larger meal

....

Rinse the *dal* in several changes of water and remove any shrivelled pieces or stones. Soak in water for 20 minutes – put a timer on to make sure it's no more. It's important that the *dal* doesn't soak for too long; you want it to retain its shape once it's cooked.

Once the 20 minutes is up, put the *dal* in a medium-sized saucepan with 250ml/8fl oz/1 cup of cold water and bring to the boil. Skim off any scum, then reduce the heat, partially cover the pan (don't fully cover it – it will boil over) and simmer for about 15 minutes or so, until the *dal* is just tender, but still holding its shape. You can arrest the cooking quickly if you need to by adding cold water to the pan.

Heat the oil in a large pan and add the garlic and chillies. Cook very gently for 1 minute, then add the *dhana jiru*, turmeric, tomatoes and salt. Bring up to the boil and simmer until the oil separates and pools around the sides of the pan. Set aside until the *moong dal* is cooked.

Put the *masala* back on the heat and bring to the boil. Tear any large spinach leaves in half, then add the spinach to the simmering *masala*. As soon as the spinach begins to wilt in the heat, add the drained *moong dal*. Cook for 10 minutes or so, until the spinach is soft, then serve immediately.

Chickpea curry
Channa nu saak

Made with canned chickpeas, this dish is lightening-quick to prepare and very tasty – perfect for an after-work supper with chappatis, *Poori* (page 116) or *Varela Parotha* (page 118), some yoghurt and a crisp, crunchy *Kachumber* (page 138). Keep a couple of cans of good-quality chickpeas in your cupboard and you'll always have this great little curry on standby.

....

2 x 400g/14oz cans chickpeas

3 cloves garlic

5mm/$^{1}/_{4}$in ginger

$^{1}/_{2}$ teaspoon salt

2 tablespoons groundnut (peanut) oil

1 medium onion, finely chopped

$^{1}/_{2}$ teaspoon finely chopped coriander (cilantro) stems

Scant $^{1}/_{2}$ teaspoon Madras curry powder

1$^{1}/_{2}$ teaspoons *dhana jiru* (page 16)

$^{1}/_{2}$ teaspoon chilli powder

$^{1}/_{4}$ teaspoon turmeric

5 tablespoons crushed canned plum tomatoes and juice

$^{1}/_{2}$ tablespoon chopped coriander (cilantro) leaves

Enough for 2 greedy people, with bread and a leafy salad

....

Drain the chickpeas of the canning liquor and rinse well. Leave to drain in a colander while you prepare the *masala*.

Crush the garlic, ginger and salt to a paste. Heat the oil in a medium-sized saucepan and add the onion. Cook gently until the onion begins to turn golden-brown. Add 3 tablespoons of water and simmer rapidly to cook the onion down to a thick paste. Reduce the heat to low and add the garlic-ginger paste and coriander stems.

When the garlic and ginger are fragrant, add the curry powder, *dhana jiru*, chilli powder and turmeric and cook briefly, taking care not to burn the spices. Add the tomatoes and 125ml/4fl oz/1 cup of water. Bring the *masala* up to simmering point and continue to simmer until the oil pools around the sides of the pan.

Add the chickpeas and 3 tablespoons of water and stir well. Cook for 10 minutes to heat the chickpeas and merge the flavours, then serve sprinkled with the coriander leaves.

Black-eyed beans curry
Chora nu saak

This recipe was given to Rose by a work colleague when she was working in a bag factory many years ago. She made friends with a Pakistani lady – they would bring in lunches to share with each other – and one day Rose's friend brought this pretty, fragrant curry for her to try. Rose loved it immediately and asked for the recipe. It contains a mixture of fennel seeds and white poppy seeds which is unique in this book – it's not used in Gujarati or East African cooking – but it adds an unusual, delicate note to the creamy beans. It has been a favourite of my wife's ever since Rose first cooked the recipe all those years ago; I adore it too, and it always goes down well with guests.

This is an excellent storecupboard standby, especially because dried black-eyed beans don't need to be soaked.

½ teaspoon fennel seeds

½ teaspoon white poppy seeds (*khus-khus*)

450g/1lb/2 cups black-eyed beans

3 tablespoons groundnut (peanut) oil

1 large onion, very finely chopped

4 cloves garlic, crushed with ½ teaspoon salt

½ teaspoon Madras curry powder

2 teaspoons *dhana jiru* (page 16)

½ teaspoon chilli powder

1 teaspoon turmeric

200ml/7fl oz crushed canned plum tomatoes and juice (about half a can)

1 tablespoon finely chopped coriander (cilantro) stems

1 tablespoon roughly chopped coriander (cilantro) leaves

Serves 6 people with rice

Use a pestle and mortar to crush the fennel and poppy seeds finely. Set the powder aside.

Wash the beans and put them in a pot with 1.5 litres/2½ pints/6 cups of cold water. Bring to the boil and cook rapidly for 10 minutes, reduce the heat and simmer for about 45 minutes until tender. Add more water as necessary.

Meanwhile, put the oil in another pan and heat moderately. Add the onion and cook until golden-brown. This will take about 10 minutes: stir frequently to avoid burning the onion at the edges of the pan. Add 4 tablespoons of water and cook rapidly until the onion forms a thick paste. Add the garlic paste, fennel and poppy seed powder, curry powder, *dhana jiru*, chilli powder and turmeric and cook for about 10 seconds, then add the tomatoes and coriander stems. Cook over medium heat until the oil pools around the sides of the pan. Set aside.

Once the beans are cooked, add them to the *masala* with any remaining cooking water. Add 750ml/1¼ pints/3 cups more water, bring to the boil and simmer for 10 minutes to combine the flavours. Sprinkle with the coriander leaves and serve with boiled basmati rice and perhaps some crunchy spring onions (scallions) to munch on.

Kidney beans curry
Janjaro nu saak

I can't say how many times this curry has come to my rescue when I've dashed home from work starving hungry, to find seemingly nothing in the house. It cooks quickly (about 15 minutes is all), and yet it has a savour and depth to it that is very satisfying. And it's simple – it's one of the few curries my wife (who claims she can't cook) makes often. All the ingredients you need for this curry can be kept in your storecupboard: you need a couple of cans of kidney beans, a can of tomatoes, your standard spices (page 16) and some onions and garlic in the house and, ideally, some chappatis, *naan* or pitta breads in the freezer. In our house we're never without these things, so we can always rustle up a tasty meal like this at very short notice.

. . . .

2 x 400g/14oz cans kidney beans

3 tablespoons groundnut (peanut) oil

1 medium onion, finely chopped

2 cloves garlic, crushed with $\frac{1}{2}$ teaspoon salt

1 teaspoon Madras curry powder

2 teaspoons *dhana jiru* (page 16)

$\frac{1}{2}$ teaspoon chilli powder

$\frac{1}{4}$ teaspoon turmeric

4 tablespoons crushed canned plum tomatoes and juice

Serves 2 with bread or rice and a leafy salad

. . . .

Drain the kidney beans and rinse them well to remove the syrupy canning liquor. Leave to drain in a colander while you make the *masala*.

Heat the oil in a medium-sized pan and add the onion. Cook over medium heat until the onion is golden-brown, then add 1 tablespoon of water and cook the onion down to a thick paste.

Add the garlic paste and cook for 15 seconds, then add the curry powder, *dhana jiru*, chilli powder and turmeric, and then the tomatoes. Simmer, stirring occasionally, until the oil pools around the sides of the pan.

Add the kidney beans (and if you want to eat this curry with rice, add 500ml/18fl oz/2 cups of water) and cook for 10 minutes to allow the flavours to merge, stirring from time to time. Serve with rice or bread, some crunchy red onion slices and yoghurt.

UNUSUALLY, there is no fresh coriander (cilantro) in our recipe for this curry. Don't be tempted to improvise in this instance and add some, even as a garnish; its flavour doesn't work well with the kidney beans – somehow, the combination gives a soapy taste.

Chickpea-flour dumplings with yoghurt
Dhokri nu saak

This curry is magic: absolutely delicious, yet made out of next to nothing! A stiff paste of *besan* (gram or chickpea flour) is cut into diamond shapes and gently simmered in a delectably creamy mixture of spices, yoghurt and tomatoes. It's sturdy stuff – you won't need bread or rice because the dumplings are quite filling.

FOR THE DUMPLINGS

Groundnut (peanut) oil for greasing

2 cloves garlic

2.5cm/1in ginger

3 green chillies

$\frac{1}{2}$ teaspoon cumin seeds

1 teaspoon salt

2 teaspoons groundnut (peanut) oil

225g/8oz/2 cups *besan* (gram or chickpea flour)

FOR THE MASALA

3 tablespoons groundnut (peanut) oil

$\frac{1}{2}$ teaspoon mustard seeds

$\frac{1}{2}$ teaspoon cumin seeds

$\frac{1}{2}$ teaspoon asafoetida

1 large onion, finely chopped

200ml/7fl oz crushed canned plum tomatoes and juice (about half a can)

2 cloves garlic, crushed with $1\frac{1}{2}$ teaspoons salt

$\frac{1}{2}$ tablespoon finely chopped coriander (cilantro) stems

1 teaspoon *dhana jiru* (page 16)

$\frac{1}{2}$ teaspoon chilli powder

$\frac{1}{4}$ teaspoon turmeric

325ml/12fl oz/$1\frac{1}{2}$ cups yoghurt

2 tablespoons chopped coriander (cilantro) leaves

Serves 4

Oil a wooden chopping board and rolling pin. Pound the garlic, ginger, chillies, cumin seeds and salt to a paste. In a medium-sized non-stick pan, bring 325ml/12fl oz/$1\frac{1}{2}$ cups of water and the garlic-ginger paste to a rolling boil. (Open a window – the steam has a potent kick!) Add 2 teaspoons of oil to the water and, when it is fully boiling, add the *besan*. Stir vigorously with a wooden spoon. Reduce the heat and cook for 3–4 minutes, stirring constantly. The mixture should now form a ball. Turn out the ball of dough onto the oiled board and roll out to a thickness of 1cm/$\frac{1}{2}$in using the oiled rolling pin. Cut across the dough in parallel lines about 3cm/$1\frac{1}{4}$in apart, then cross through to make diamond shapes. Set aside.

To make the *masala*, heat the oil gently in a large pan and add the mustard and cumin seeds. Infuse for a minute, then add the asafoetida. Cook for a few seconds, add the onion, then increase the heat. Cook until the onion begins to turn golden, then add the tomatoes, garlic paste, coriander stems, *dhana jiru*, chilli powder and turmeric. Bring up to a simmer and cook until the oil pools around the sides of the pan.

Mix the yoghurt with 250ml/8fl oz/1 cup of water. When the *masala* is cooked, stir in the yoghurt. Increase the heat and stir constantly until the mixture boils, or it will curdle. Add the dumplings, stirring them through the *masala* carefully. Simmer gently for 5 minutes to heat through and serve sprinkled with coriander.

Brown lentil curry
Masoor nu saak

This is unassuming-sounding, but very good. Plain old brown lentils (it's very good with whole green lentils too) are cooked in a thick, reduced *masala*, to eat with bread: this is classic *Khoja* cooking. *Masoor nu saak* is even better if you cook it the day before you want to eat it, or if you have leftovers the next day. Serve just as it is with warm chappatis, sliced onions, yoghurt and Lemon Salt Pickle (page 126), for a wholesome and tasty light lunch.

8oz/250g/1 cup whole *masoor* (whole brown lentils)

2 fat cloves garlic

1cm/$\frac{1}{2}$in ginger

1 teaspoon salt

2 tablespoons olive oil

$\frac{1}{4}$ teaspoon mustard seeds

Large pinch of fenugreek seeds

$\frac{1}{2}$ teaspoon *dhana jiru* (page 16)

$\frac{1}{2}$ teaspoon chilli powder

$\frac{1}{2}$ teaspoon turmeric

200ml/7fl oz crushed canned plum tomatoes and juice (about half a can)

Lemon juice to taste (optional)

Serves 2 with chappatis

Wash the lentils in hot water and pick out any shrivelled bits or stones. Put the drained lentils into a small pan with 750ml/1$\frac{1}{4}$ pints/3 cups of water and bring to the boil. Simmer rapidly for 10 minutes then reduce the heat. Simmer gently until the lentils are tender – this can take anything from 20–40 minutes, depending on the freshness of your batch of lentils. Watch carefully to ensure they don't boil dry – add more boiling water as you need to.

Meanwhile, pound the garlic, ginger and salt to a paste. Put the oil in a pan and place over gentle heat. Add the mustard and fenugreek seeds, then the garlic-ginger paste and cook gently for a minute or so. Add the *dhana jiru*, chilli powder and turmeric, cook for a few seconds only, then add the tomatoes.

Bring up to the boil and simmer, stirring frequently, until the oil separates and pools around the sides of the pan. Set aside until the lentils are cooked.

Drain the lentils and add them to the pan of *masala*. Stir well and cook gently for 5 minutes to combine the flavours. Taste and add a little lemon juice to perk up the flavours if you need to – just a little, you don't want the flavour of the lemon to dominate – and serve hot.

White lentils in spiced yoghurt
Dai vari urad ni daar

Pale and interesting sums up this *dal* – ivory-coloured lentils in a subtly spiced yoghurt sauce with a clean, fresh flavour. It's a classic Gujarati dish, brought to Uganda by Rose's mother, and loved especially by Sultan, one of Rose's older brothers. It's lovely with Millet Flatbread (page 117), as part of a larger meal. Serve the *dal* in small bowls – then do as Rose advises: break your *rotlo* into pieces, drop it into your *dal* and eat with a spoon.

225g/8oz/1 cup *urad dal* (split black lentils – note that these will be white because they have had their husks removed)

1 fat clove garlic

3 green chillies

$\frac{1}{2}$ teaspoon cumin seeds

$\frac{1}{2}$ teaspoon salt

$\frac{1}{4}$ teaspoon turmeric

250ml/8fl oz/1 cup yoghurt

1 tablespoon finely chopped coriander (cilantro) leaves

Serves 4 as a side dish

Wash and drain the lentils. Place in a medium-sized pan with 1.5 litres/$2\frac{1}{2}$ pints/6 cups of water, bring up to simmering point and cook until completely soft – for about 30 minutes or so. Turn off the heat and beat the lentils with a whisk to make a smooth, soupy purée – or blend briefly with a hand-held blender.

Crush the garlic, chillies, cumin seeds and salt to a paste. Add them to the *dal* with the turmeric and stir well.

Mix the yoghurt with 125ml/4fl oz/$\frac{1}{2}$ cup of water. Add it to the *dal*, stir well, then place the pan over medium heat. Stir constantly – if you don't, the yoghurt will curdle – as you bring the mixture back up to the boil. Cook for a few minutes to heat the yoghurt through, then serve sprinkled with the coriander leaves.

Breads

It's a sad state of affairs, but in these times of increased wealth and so-called quality of life, most of us find little time for such simple daily pleasures as freshly made bread. In Indian households – especially Northern Indian homes, where bread is traditionally more important than rice – it's a different story: no self-respecting Indian housewife would offer a meal without a stack of freshly homemade, piping-hot breads. Indian breads are best made fresh each day: while curries simmer, dough (usually unleavened) is prepared, rolled and quickly cooked on the *tava*, a curved cast-iron stove-top griddle. Indian flatbreads are essential not just for the nutritional balance and bulk they bring to the meal – they're also used in the mechanical process of eating. Using the right hand's fingertips only, diners tear a portion of bread from the round and use it to scoop up a little of their curry. A well-cooked bread should be supple and light, perfectly containing – but not dominating – each mouthful, while the comforting texture and mild, wheaty taste complement any spicy-hot, intensely flavoured dish.

FRESHLY COOKED BREADS, such as these *poori*, served *garam-garam* – piping hot, fresh, and fragrant from the *tava* or frying pan (skillet) – are one of the greatest pleasures of Indian home cooking, and a treat that is served up daily. Indian mums the world over will get their families to the table before beginning to cook their breads: as each batch is cooked, it is handed out to the family in strict rotation so that everyone can enjoy the bread in peak condition.

Chappatis
Rotli

These unleavened flatbreads are a cornerstone of the Gujarati diet – *rotli* (chappatis) and *saak* (curry) are served up most nights of the week. An Indian housewife's prowess is judged by, among other things, the quality of her *rotli*. After years of making them, Rose can turn them out at impressive speed, each perfectly round and of identical size to the last. While it takes a while to be able to turn out *rotli* as perfect as Rose's, I urge you to have a go – they're not difficult and are far nicer (and cost less) than ready-made. *Rotli* reheat well from frozen (for details on how to freeze, see the note on page 118), so if you're going to the effort of making some, make a big batch and freeze a few for another day. Leftover chappatis are often eaten for breakfast, fried until crisp and accompanied by a cup of tea.

....

350g/12oz/2 cups wholemeal (whole-wheat) flour, plus extra for dusting
Pinch of salt
2½ tablespoons sunflower oil

Makes 8
....

Mix the flour, salt and oil thoroughly by hand, then add 250–300ml/8–10fl oz/1–1¼ cups of boiling water and mix with a wooden spoon. Add more water gradually until you have a soft, pliable dough. Work the mixture with the spoon until the dough is cool enough to handle, then knead for a minute or so. Divide the mixture into 8 and roll each portion into a flattened ball between your palms, pressing hard.

Dust your work surface with flour and put some into a small bowl. Dip the first ball into the flour before rolling evenly into a 20cm/8in round, without turning over. Roll as many as you can accommodate on your work surface, then begin cooking the breads. (A rest between rolling and cooking improves the chances of the *rotli* puffing up when cooked, which makes it light.)

Heat a *tava* or frying pan (skillet) on a high heat. When hot, place a round of rolled-out dough face-down on the pan. Leave for 10–20 seconds, then flip. If the pan is at the right temperature, you'll see light spots of brown on the surface of the *rotli*. Leave for 30–40 seconds (in the meantime, roll another *rotli*), then flip again.

Press the surface lightly with a spatula (Rose has a special wooden 'mushroom' for this job). With any luck, the *rotli* should begin to puff up – large bubbles will appear under the surface. Let the bubbles swell up nicely: if you see any steam escaping, use your spatula to try to block the steam's escape. As steam builds up inside the *rotli*, it will puff. Take care: escaping steam will be scaldingly hot. This stage shouldn't take longer than 20 seconds – any longer will make the *rotli* dry and stiff. Remove the *rotli* to a plate, placing it face-down. Repeat with the remaining dough rounds – rolling out more as you go. Stack the cooked breads neatly, one on top of the other, to keep them warm. Serve as soon as you're finished, or cover with a tea towel and cool thoroughly before freezing.

»see pictures on the following pages

Thick whole-wheat flatbreads
Bhakri

When Rose was a girl, her family's main meal of the day was always at lunchtime. In the evenings they would have a fairly light snack, such as this bread. It's thick and unleavened, and eaten hot from the griddle, well buttered and accompanied by some yoghurt and pickles. *Bhakri* are quite filling; they make a good, fortifying breakfast (you won't need elevenses – we often have them if we're off on a journey). One essential accompaniment *bhakri* cannot be served without is a good, hot cup of tea.

350g/12oz/2 cups wholemeal (whole-wheat) flour, plus extra for dusting
1½ teaspoons salt
2½ tablespoons sunflower oil
4 tablespoons butter

Makes 4 *bhakri*

Put the flour, salt and oil together in a large bowl and mix thoroughly by hand. Slowly add 60–125ml/2–4fl oz/¼–½ cup of water – just enough to bring the mixture together to make a dryish ball of dough. Use the ball of dough to pick up any loose crumbs in the bowl, then divide it into 4 equal portions.

Before rolling out, set a *tava* or heavy-based 23cm/9in frying pan (skillet) over medium heat.

Squash each portion of the dough into a ball, kneading it well to amalgamate it. Sprinkle your work surface with flour and dust your rolling pin, then roll one ball out into a round about 5mm/½in thick. The edge will be rugged and broken-looking, but don't worry – that's how it should be. Repeat with the remaining dough.

When you've rolled out all the balls of dough, put the first round face-down on the hot pan. Leave it for 30 seconds, then flip it over. Let the underside cook nicely and evenly (you may want to spin the bread on the pan from time to time to ensure even cooking) and, when it is spotted with brown, turn it over again and cook the other side in the same way. The whole process should take about 2 minutes – if it takes more or less time, adjust your heat accordingly. As soon as the bread is done, remove it to a plate and spread the butter all over the top surface. Cook the other dough rounds in the same way and eat them while they're hot and glistening with melted butter.

Spiced flatbreads with fenugreek
Masala parotha

The very first thing I ever ate in India, for breakfast early one December morning after a long overnight flight into Delhi, was a stack of breads like these. They were served with curd (India's thick, rich yoghurt), hot lime pickle, fruit juice and hot *chai* (*masala* tea). They were delicious. The stress of air travel was gone: with my belly full, I settled down happily for a power nap, knowing it was going to be a good trip.

These breads have a spicy, resinous aroma imparted by fresh fenugreek leaves, which may be found in supermarkets (especially if there is an Indian or Pakistani community nearby). Or try an Asian grocer's – but if you can't find them, leave them out: the breads will still taste good.

....

700g/1½lb/4 cups wholemeal
(whole-wheat) flour

¼ bunch of fresh fenugreek (about a handful)

2 fat cloves garlic

2 green chillies

1 teaspoon cumin seeds

1¼ teaspoons salt

1 tablespoon finely chopped coriander
(cilantro) leaves

¼ teaspoon turmeric

1½ teaspoons sesame seeds

2 tablespoons oil, plus extra for brushing

Makes 6 *parotha*

....

First, remove some bran from the wholemeal flour: sieve the flour into a large bowl and discard the bran left in the sieve. Take 350g/12oz/2 cups of the sifted flour to make the breads and keep the rest to one side for dusting the work surface and rolling pin (and any left at the end can be put back into the bag).

Wash the fenugreek, pick the leaves and discard the stems. Finely chop the leaves. Pound the garlic, chillies, cumin seeds and salt to a paste.

Add the oil to the flour in the bowl and mix by hand to a fine, crumbly mixture. Add the fenugreek, coriander, garlic-chilli paste, turmeric and sesame seeds and mix well. Gradually add warm water – roughly 150ml/5fl oz/⅔ cup – to make a stiff but workable dough. Knead briefly, then divide the dough into 6 portions.

Roll each portion into a flattened ball between your palms, pressing hard. Flour your surface and rolling pin with some of the remaining sifted flour. Set a heavy-based 23cm/9in frying pan (skillet) or *tava* over medium heat while you roll out the breads. Put a dish of oil and a pastry brush by the stove, ready for cooking the breads.

Roll each round of dough, without turning over, into an 18cm/7in circle. To cook, place one face-down on the hot pan. Cook for 30 seconds and turn over. Brush the top lightly with oil, then turn over again, and brush the other side with oil. When the underside is patched with golden-brown, flip the bread and cook the other side to the same degree. Remove to a plate lined with kitchen paper and repeat the process with the other dough rounds. Stack the breads as you remove them from the pan to keep them warm and soft. Serve immediately, or freeze. (For details on freezing, see the note on page 118.)

Pitta-style breads
Naan

Making *naan* is fun; they're probably the easiest breads to make in the book and yet they look impressive. As with *Poori* (page 116), it's very gratifying to see bread doing what it should – swelling and puffing before your very eyes. These work best with a combination of dry-frying and a fierce blast from an overhead grill (broiler) – preheat yours for a while before you cook. The result is light, soft, yeasty little pockets of bread, delicious served warm with kebabs, barbecued meats or roast lamb. A stack of freshly made *naan* is the ideal accompaniment to *Kalyo* (page 60) – or, for vegetarians, Cauliflower, Potato and Pea Curry (page 30) or Pea Curry (page 32). Like the other breads in the chapter, *naan* freeze and reheat nicely. (For details on how to freeze, see the note on page 118.)

....

450g/1lb strong white bread flour, plus
extra for dusting

1 teaspoon salt

1 teaspoon caster (superfine) sugar

1 sachet easy-blend dried yeast

1 tablespoon groundnut (peanut) oil

Makes 16

....

Put the dry ingredients into a large mixing bowl. Add the oil and about 275ml/½ pint/1 cup of warm water (precise amounts depend on your flour) to make a soft, pliable dough. Place in an oiled bowl, cover with clingfilm (plastic wrap) and leave in a warm place to rise for half an hour or so, until the dough has doubled in size.

Remove the dough to a floured surface. Knead vigorously for 2–3 minutes, then put the dough back into the oiled bowl and return it to the warm place to double in size again.

Knead the dough again, then divide into 16 portions. Roll each portion into a ball.

Flour your work surface and rolling pin. Roll out the balls of dough into ovals, about 18cm/7in long and 10cm/4in wide.

Now prepare to cook the breads. Set a heavy-based frying pan (skillet) or *tava* over medium-high heat and preheat an overhead grill (broiler) to its highest setting. Set a baking sheet (cookie sheet) under the grill to preheat and lightly dampen a clean tea towel to put the breads in once they're cooked (this helps them stay soft).

To cook the breads, it's best to deal with them one at a time. Put one into the frying pan or *tava* and cook until the underside is lightly mottled with brown and you can see bubbles beginning to form under the surface.

Lift the bread out of the pan and put it under the grill (uncooked side uppermost) and watch like a hawk while it swells up dramatically – this happens quickly and, with the temperature so high, there is a risk of the bread burning, so pay attention. Cook until just turning the palest golden-brown, then whip the *naan* out and wrap it in the damp tea towel. Cook the other breads in the same way, making a stack enclosed in the tea towel. Serve them warm, or allow to cool fully before freezing.

Balloon breads
Poori

Poori (pictured on page 107) are spectacular –
the way these little rounds of the simplest flour-
and-water dough magically balloon up when
they hit the hot oil never fails to impress me. If
you've had *poori* in restaurants before and found
them flabby or greasy, don't be put off – Rose's
recipe ensures light, un-greasy results. Just take
care, as ever, when deep-frying: never leave the
pan unattended, and never fill it to more than
a third of its depth with oil.

   Poori are wonderful served hot with *Shikhan*
(page 184), but also good with any dry vegetable
curry. When my wife, Salima, was growing up,
poori were served for weekend breakfast as a
treat. The breads would be set in the centre of
the table in a giant, battered stainless-steel bowl,
with separate dishes of yoghurt, crushed garlic,
crushed cumin seeds and pounded green
chillies arranged around it. Each member of
the family would mix a yoghurt chutney to their
own liking to accompany their *poori*. However
you choose to serve them, *poori* are best eaten
as soon after they're cooked as possible – they
deflate as they cool – so get your diners to the
table and serve your beautiful breads hot,
straight from the pan in all their puffed-up glory.

525g/1lb 2oz/3 cups wholemeal
(whole-wheat) flour
$\frac{1}{2}$ teaspoon salt
2 tablespoons groundnut (peanut) oil, plus
more for deep-frying

Makes 12–14 *poori*

Sift the wholemeal flour and discard the bran
left in the sieve. Measure out 350g/12oz/2 cups
of the resulting paler flour into a bowl and set
the rest aside for dusting later on.

Add the oil and salt to the flour in the bowl and
work the mixture with your fingers until evenly
combined. Add around 125ml/4fl oz/$\frac{1}{2}$ cup of
cold water, just enough to bring the mixture
together to make a stiff but pliable dough.

Knead briefly, then divide into walnut-sized
balls – you should have 12–14.

Dust your work surface and rolling pin with the
reserved flour and roll out each piece of dough
to a round of about 12cm/5in in diameter. Don't
turn the dough over during the rolling.

Fill a wok or *karai* to a third of its depth with oil
and set over high heat. To tell if the oil is ready
for cooking, test the temperature by dropping in
a crumb of dough – it should float immediately,
surrounded by bubbles.

Pick up a round of dough and pass it quickly
from hand to hand to shake off any excess flour.
Slide it carefully into the oil, then quickly take a
slotted spoon and use it to push the bread down
just below the surface of the oil. It should puff
up dramatically – once the bread is fully puffed,
turn it over with the spoon to cook the other side
to a golden-brown colour. Remove to a plate
lined with kitchen paper and fry the other
breads in the same way. Serve hot.

Millet flatbread
Bajra no rotlo

During her childhood in Uganda, Rose's family grew millet and milled the dark red grains in a heavy hand-turned millstone. The resulting light grey flour was used mainly to make this dense, nutritious bread with its distinctive, faintly bitter taste. Rose loved this bread and often asked her mother to cook it, whereupon she would be told, "You grind the millet and I'll make you *rotla*." Making bread with freshly milled *bajra* flour sounds like luxury to me, especially as it doesn't keep well – the flavour deteriorates rapidly, so buy only a little at a time.

Rotla (the plural of *rotlo*) are traditionally served with White Lentils in Spiced Yoghurt (page 105) and Bitter Gourd with Onions (page 37). The unusual flavours of these dishes work well with the bread. They are also good as a snack with yoghurt and pickle or chutney.

....

175g/6oz/1 cup *bajra* (millet) flour
1 tablespoon plain (all-purpose) flour
$\frac{1}{2}$ teaspoon salt
2 tablespoons cold butter
Groundnut (peanut) oil for greasing

Makes 1 *rotlo*
....

Put the flours and salt in a large mixing bowl. Set half a tablespoon of the butter aside, then add the remaining butter to the bowl. Using your fingertips, lightly rub the butter into the flour until the mixture looks like breadcrumbs. While you do this, lift your hands up high to aerate the flour as it falls back into the bowl.

Little by little, add warm water and stir with a wooden spoon to make a soft, pliable but not sticky dough – you'll probably need to add about 75ml/3fl oz/$\frac{1}{3}$ cup. Knead energetically until the dough begins to feel firmer and silkier – and a little bit sticky. Lightly oil a heavy-based frying pan (skillet) or *tava* and set over low heat.

Take a piece of greaseproof (waxed) paper, about 30cm/12in square, and sprinkle lightly with water. Place the dough in the centre of the paper. Wet a rolling pin and roll out the dough to a 15cm/6in circle. Then, using your hands, spread the dough out as evenly as you can to make the circle about 18cm/7in in diameter. Don't worry if the top looks slightly bumpy – that's how it's meant to be.

Have a small container of water and a pastry brush ready at the side of the stove. Slip your hand under the paper and lift up the dough. Firmly place the dough face-down on the pan (Rose slams it down and always gets it bang on centre!) and peel the paper off the top. Brush the top with water – paying particular attention to the edges, where it can crack if it gets too dry.

When the bread begins to swell and bubble, turn it over – the underside should be touched here and there with golden-brown. Continue cooking until the other side has golden-brown spots. Give the bread a little press here and there with a spatula – if you're lucky it will puff up. As soon as it's cooked, remove it to a warm plate and rub the remaining butter over the surface of the hot bread to melt it. Serve immediately.

Flaky flatbreads
Varela parotha

If you enjoyed playing with Play-Doh as a child, you'll love making these breads. A simple white unleavened dough is enriched with butter and artfully rolled to create separated, flaky layers. Serve *parotha* with Prawn Curry (page 52) or Lamb with Saffron and Yoghurt (page 60), or try them with butter and honey – a favourite breakfast treat of my late father-in-law.

700g/1½lb/4 cups strong white bread flour, plus extra for dusting
2½ teaspoons salt
4 tablespoons sunflower oil, plus extra for brushing
50g/2oz/¼ cup butter, melted

Makes 8 breads

Put the flour and salt in a bowl and add enough water to make a stiff dough – you'll probably need about 325ml/12fl oz/1½ cups. Knead for about 5 minutes until the mixture becomes smooth and elastic, and is no longer sticky.

Divide the mixture into 8 and roll each piece firmly into a ball between your palms. Flour a work surface and rolling pin and roll out one ball of dough into a round until it is about 2mm/⅛in thick. Brush the top very generously with butter and sprinkle lightly with flour.

Roll the round from the edge into a tight sausage shape (see picture on page 120, top right). As you roll, pull the sausage out along its length to stretch it a little. Starting at one end of the sausage, roll it up into a tight, flat coil (see

page 120, bottom left). Tuck the tail end into the centre of the coil (see page 120, bottom right), then lay the coil down on the floured surface and squash to make a slightly flattened but still circular disc.

Take the rolling pin and roll lightly and gradually, without turning over, until you have a 18cm/7in circle. Take care to keep an even thickness – draw your hand across the surface to see if there are any thicker parts and even them out with the rolling pin. Repeat this process with the other portions of dough.

Put a heavy-based frying pan (skillet) – one large enough to take the breads – or *tava* over a lowish heat and, when it's heated, place a bread face-down on it. Brush lightly with oil, then turn the bread over. Brush on the other side and cook until the underside is patched with golden-brown and flaky. Turn and cook until the other side is golden-brown too. Remove to a plate and cover with a tea towel while you cook the other breads in the same way, stacking them as you go. Serve hot, or leave to cool before freezing.

»see pictures on the following pages

TO FREEZE, cool the breads completely and stack them interleaved with greaseproof (waxed) paper, before slipping them into a freezer bag and placing them flat in the freezer. To reheat from frozen, heat gently in your frying pan (skillet) or *tava*, turning the bread frequently until piping hot.

Chutneys, pickles and relishes

The traditions of preserving and pickling are strong in Indian culture and, although those techniques are less essential for survival than they once were, the special flavours produced by these ancient methods are still highly valued. No special-occasion meal would be complete without an array of condiments being offered to guests. Chutneys, pickles and relishes offer a contrast of flavour and texture to the main dishes: crisp, juicy and cooling, salty and sharp, or pungent and sour. Some condiments work particularly well with certain foods and have become traditional accompaniments: *akhni*, that gently spiced pilau of meat, potatoes and rice, is unimaginable without a crunchy, zesty *kachumber*. Crisply fried, sizzling-hot *bhajia* would seem incomplete without a dipping sauce of dark, sour-sweet *ambli*. Offer any of these recipes when you want to distinguish a meal from the everyday: a carefully chosen pickle, chutney or relish can make any meal instantly more special.

A TRAY OF PICKLES gives diners the opportunity to customise their plate of food to suit their own palates. Those with a taste for extra heat can choose pickled chillies or green chutney; those wishing to cool the fire can select either *raitha* or *bhartu*. Try this ingenious way to please all of your guests: select accompaniments from this chapter that will enhance and counterbalance the flavours of the main dishes.

Aubergine purée with chilli and onions
Bhartu

There are two recipes here – one for a hot dish, served in winter with a thick bread such as *Bajra no Rotlo* (page 117) or *Bhakri* (page 112), and another that is served cold as a dip to accompany barbecue foods in the summer. Both are tasty and useful – the contrast of textures these dishes provide is a good supplement to many meals.

2 medium-sized aubergines (eggplants)
Groundnut (peanut) oil for brushing

TO SERVE HOT

1 clove garlic
1 green chilli, trimmed and roughly chopped
½ teaspoon salt
10g/½oz/1 tablespoon butter
1 small onion, very finely chopped
1 tablespoon chopped coriander (cilantro) leaves

TO SERVE COLD

125ml/4fl oz/½ cup Greek-style (plain, strained) yoghurt
1 clove garlic, crushed
1 green chilli, finely chopped
3 spring onions (scallions), finely chopped
½ tablespoon chopped coriander (cilantro) leaves

Makes enough for 4 servings as a dip with breads, or more as part of a larger meal

For both versions, you need to start by cooking the aubergines. Preheat an overhead grill (broiler) to its highest setting. Brush a baking sheet (cookie sheet) with oil.

Trim the sepals from the aubergines (see picture on page 26, top left) and prick the aubergines here and there with a fork. Brush them with oil and lay them on the baking sheet. Grill (broil) them, turning frequently, until they're completely soft. Allow them to cool a little, then peel off the skin and discard. Chop the flesh into cubes and mash thoroughly with a fork. Then:

To serve hot, crush the garlic with the chilli and salt to a paste. Heat the butter in a frying pan (skillet) and add the onion. Cook gently until the onion is beginning to soften. Add the garlic-chilli paste and fry gently for half a minute before adding the mashed aubergine flesh. Cook briefly to heat through, then scatter with the coriander leaves and serve hot.

To serve cold, mix the cooled aubergine purée with the yoghurt, garlic, chilli and spring onions. Chill thoroughly until you are ready to serve, then sprinkle with the coriander leaves.

Mustard-pickled chillies
Rai vara mircha

If you can get hold of the split mustard seeds required for this recipe, it's a doddle. This key ingredient may take some tracking down – you could try online if you're not near an Indian supermarket or grocer. Of course, this pickle is for the chilli addicts out there, who want a little fieriness with their food. The mustard flavour is delicious with many vegetable dishes and *dal*.

200g/7oz very fresh green chillies

50g/2oz split mustard seeds

Juice of 2 lemons

4 teaspoons salt

$\frac{1}{2}$ teaspoon turmeric

3 tablespoons sunflower oil

2 teaspoons fennel seeds, crushed (optional)

Makes enough to fill one 750g/1½lb jar

Wash and thoroughly dry the chillies, then top and tail them. Split each chilli in half along its length and put them in a large bowl. Crush the mustard seeds and add them to the chillies with the lemon juice, salt, turmeric, oil and fennel seeds (if using). Mix well and cover. Leave to stand in a cool place for 24 hours.

Sterilise your jar by rinsing it carefully in boiling water. Leave it to dry upside down on a clean tea towel. When it is completely dry, pack the chillies and the spicy lemon juice into the jar. Leave in a cool place for 1 week before eating and, once open, store in the fridge.

HOMEMADE PICKLES made without chemical preservatives keep best if, once opened, you don't leave the jar out of the fridge for any length of time. When you want to eat some pickle, take a little out of the jar – put it into a bowl for your table – and put the jar straight back in the fridge. Never put any leftovers back into the jar. In this way your pickle should keep nicely in the fridge for several weeks.

Lemon salt pickle
Limbu nu anthnu

Sharp and salty, this is a perfect piquant accompaniment to rich curries and *dal* dishes. I particularly love it when it's made with a root known variously as *amba haldi* (in Hindi), *amber hurder* (in Gujarati), mango turmeric or mango ginger. As you might expect from the English names, it has a lovely mango-like flavour. It can be tricky to find; it's usually available only in winter, and only in very good Indian (most likely, Gujarati) grocers. If you do manage to track some down, try it – but if you can't get this or the slightly more common turmeric root, leave them out altogether. The pickle will still taste fantastic. (For identification purposes, look at the picture on page 128, bottom left: *amber hurder* is in the small dish to the left and turmeric root is on the small plate to the right.)

Use a 1-litre (1-quart) glass clip-top preserving jar for this, or sterilise a few empty jam jars. To maximise the length of time the pickle will keep, see my note on page 125.

4 whole lemons
5cm/2in ginger, scraped clean
15cm/6in *amber hurder* (optional), scraped clean
10cm/4in turmeric root (optional), scraped clean
Juice of 4 lemons (plus extra if required)
8 green chillies
4 tablespoons salt
½ teaspoon turmeric

Makes enough to fill a 1-litre (1-quart) jar

Boil a large pan of water and wash the jar, the whole lemons, the roots (if you're using them), the chillies, a sharp knife for chopping, a chopping board, a large non-reactive mixing bowl and a metal spoon for mixing.

Cut the ginger into 5mm-/¼in-thick slices and, if you're using the turmeric root or *amber hurder*, cut them into small rounds (see picture on page 128, bottom left). Put the cut roots into the sterilised mixing bowl.

Cut the tips off the whole lemons, then cut them into 8 wedges. Cut away any thicker pieces of membrane and discard, then cut the wedges into 2.5cm/1in pieces (see page 128, bottom right). Add the pieces to the roots in the bowl.

Cut a slit along the length of each of the chillies. Add them to the lemon and roots in the bowl and scatter the salt and turmeric over the top. Pour in the lemon juice and mix well with the sterilised spoon to dissolve the salt.

Pack the mixture into the jar, pushing everything down to ensure it is fully submerged in the juice (add more lemon juice to top up the level if you need to). Clip on the lid and leave the jar in a sunny spot for 2–3 days. The pickle is now ready to eat – keep it in the refrigerator and it will last for a couple of months or so.

»see pictures on the following pages

Yoghurt with cucumber and mustard
Raitha

Good with grilled meats, tandoori foods, *Akhni* (pages 82–84) and anything else you fancy, this dish is a useful one to serve when you are unsure of your guests' ability to deal with chilli heat. Even when the green chilli is included in the relish, the yoghurt and cucumber have a fantastic cooling effect on the palate – but leave the chilli out altogether if you fear your guests are not chilli veterans! Make it at the last minute: over time, the cucumber leaks its juices into the yoghurt, and makes the *raitha* thin – so it won't keep for any length of time.

Makes enough for 6–8 people

1 small cucumber (or half a large one)

500ml/18fl oz Greek-style (plain, strained) yoghurt

$\frac{1}{2}$ teaspoon powdered mustard

1 clove garlic, crushed with $\frac{1}{2}$ teaspoon salt

3 spring onions (scallions), trimmed, green and white parts finely sliced

$\frac{1}{2}$ green chilli, finely chopped (optional)

1 tablespoon chopped coriander (cilantro)

If the cucumber is organic, you don't need to peel it; otherwise thinly pare away the skin. Coarsely grate the cucumber, then add it to the yoghurt with the other ingredients. Stir well and serve immediately.

Tomato and chilli chutney
Lal chatni

An essential accompaniment to *Dhokra* (page 151), *Bhajia* (page 143) and *Chilla* (page 157), this is spicy and tart-sweet. Use good-quality ketchup: try to find one that isn't too sugary – it will make all the difference here.

Enough for 4 people

3 cloves garlic

$\frac{1}{2}$ teaspoon cumin seeds

$\frac{1}{2}$ teaspoon salt

$\frac{3}{4}$ teaspoon chilli powder

3 tablespoons crushed canned plum tomatoes and juice

1 tablespoon tomato ketchup

3 tablespoons lemon juice

1 tablespoon sunflower oil

1 teaspoon chopped coriander (cilantro)

Pound the garlic, cumin seeds and salt to make a paste. Add the tomatoes, chilli powder, ketchup, lemon juice, oil and coriander and stir well.

Coconut chutney
Narial ni chatni

For this recipe, you need only half a coconut, so I suggest you freeze the remaining half for another time. If you're going to eat the chutney immediately, the yoghurt makes a tasty addition (but if you don't expect to eat it all up on the same day, leave out the yoghurt and the chutney will keep in the fridge for 4–5 days). It's wonderful with many of the snacks in this book, particularly *Chilla* (page 157).

1 fresh coconut

½ bunch of coriander (cilantro), leaves picked and roughly chopped, and a handful of the stems finely chopped

3 green chillies, topped and tailed, and cut into short lengths

Juice of half a lemon

1 teaspoon salt

125ml/4fl oz/½ cup yoghurt (optional)

Makes enough for 6–8 people

First deal with your coconut. Find the softest of the three 'eyes' (the black dots located at one end of the shell). Poke it out with a skewer or slender knife and widen the hole as much as you can with the tip of a knife. Then sit the coconut on top of a wide glass or jug to allow the juice to drain away. You can strain and drink this (Rose always gave this to my wife when she was a girl – she still loves it).

When no more liquid runs out, wrap the coconut in a tea towel, then put it into a clean polythene bag and bash it with a hammer or smash it against a hard floor or pavement. (You're aiming to break the coconut into manageable-sized pieces – don't get carried away and smash it to smithereens.) Pick the pieces out of the tea towel, then carefully prise the flesh away from the shell with a knife. Pare away the brown outer coating on the flesh with a potato peeler and wipe the chunks of flesh with damp paper to remove any fibres or fragments of shell.

Set half of the flesh aside for another use – it freezes well. Put the rest into a blender with the coriander, chillies, lemon juice and 250ml/8fl oz/1 cup of water. Blend until smooth and, if you're going to eat straight away, add the yoghurt. Stir well and serve.

Green mango and coriander chutney
Lili chatni

If you ever see beautifully waxen, unripe green baby mangoes in the shops, buy some and make this tart, spicy chutney. It's particularly good with *Bhajia* (page 143) or *Hondwo* (page 154).

2 small green mangoes
1 bunch of coriander (cilantro), washed well
3 green chillies, trimmed and roughly chopped
1 clove garlic
1 tablespoon groundnut (peanut) oil
$\frac{1}{2}$ teaspoon salt
About 20 raw peanuts, peeled (optional)

Makes enough for 4–6 people

Pare the skin from the mangoes, then halve and stone them. Around the area where the stone was, there will be a layer of white pith; pull this away and discard it, then chop the mango flesh into smallish cubes, roughly 1cm/$\frac{1}{2}$in.

Roughly chop the coriander stems and leaves. Put them into the goblet of a blender with the mango flesh, chillies, garlic, oil, salt and peanuts (if you are using them). Add 125ml/4fl oz/$\frac{1}{2}$ cup of water and blend to a smooth paste.

Coriander chutney
Lila dhana ni chatni

This hot chutney adds a fresh, almost citrus note to fried dishes. It's good with Minced Lamb Kebabs (page 64) and *Mishkaki* (page 65), and I prefer it to the more usual tomato chutney with *Dhokra* (page 151).

1 bunch of coriander (cilantro), washed well
1 clove garlic, roughly chopped
4 green chillies, trimmed and roughly chopped
$\frac{1}{2}$ teaspoon salt
3 tablespoons lemon juice
$\frac{1}{2}$ teaspoon caster (superfine) sugar
1 tablespoon groundnut (peanut) oil (optional)

Makes enough for 4–6 people

Chop the whole bunch of coriander roughly – stems, roots (if any) and all (make sure that everything is carefully washed first to remove sand and grit). Put it into a blender goblet and add the garlic, chillies, salt, lemon juice and sugar. Blend to a fine paste. If the mixture sticks, add a couple of tablespoons of water.

If you plan to eat the chutney the same day, you don't need to add any oil, but if you think it may hang around in the fridge, stir in the oil and it should keep well for 3–4 days.

Tamarind chutney
Ambli ni chatni

The rich, sweet-and-sour flavour of tamarind might be familiar to you if you like HP or Worcestershire sauce: it's an important ingredient in both. *Ambli ni chatni* is served with many fried snacks and grilled meats, helping to lubricate as much as enhance flavour. You can buy tamarind in its natural state in pods, dried in compressed blocks, or as a concentrated extract. For this recipe you can use the compressed block or the concentrate. (If you happen to find the concentrate, it's much easier to deal with.) It's hard to make a smaller quantity than this, but the basic tamarind juice does freeze well.

FOR THE TAMARIND WATER

200g/7oz block of compressed tamarind, or 3 tablespoons concentrated extract

1 teaspoon salt

6 dried dates (if you're using a compressed block of tamarind)

2 tablespoons brown sugar (if you are using the concentrate)

TO SERVE (ENOUGH FOR 4 PEOPLE)

1 green chilli, finely chopped, or $\frac{1}{4}$ teaspoon chilli powder

$\frac{1}{2}$ tablespoon finely chopped red onion (optional)

$\frac{1}{2}$ tablespoon finely grated carrot (optional)

1 teaspoon finely chopped coriander (cilantro) leaves (optional)

Makes enough for 4 people

First, make up a batch of tamarind water:

If you are using tamarind block, break it into small pieces and put in a small pan with 750ml/1$\frac{1}{4}$ pints/3 cups of water, the salt and the dates. Bring to the boil and cook rapidly for 15 minutes, then reduce the heat and simmer for 5 minutes. The tamarind pulp should be very soft. Pour the contents of the pan into a sieve suspended over a bowl and press to extract as much of the pulp as possible. Discard the tangle of fibres and seeds left in the sieve. To the sieved pulp in the bowl, add 250ml/8fl oz/1 cup of cold water, stir well and leave to cool.

If you are using the concentrate, mix it with 750ml/1$\frac{1}{4}$ pints/3 cups of hot water and the sugar until thoroughly blended. Add 250ml/8fl oz/1 cup of cold water and set aside.

To serve, use 125ml/4fl oz/$\frac{1}{2}$ cup of tamarind water mixed with the chilli or chilli powder. You can serve it just like that or, for a fancier version that's particularly good with *bhajia*, add the onion, carrot and coriander.

The leftover tamarind water, made by either method, will freeze well: pour into ice-cube trays or divide into 125ml/4fl oz/$\frac{1}{2}$-cup batches. Defrost as required.

Stuffed chillies
Bharela mircha

Those with a taste for the peppery flavour and heat of green chillies will enjoy these delicious, fiery little morsels. Be warned: they are very hot! You can take the edge off their heat a little by scooping out the seeds from inside the chillies, but if you don't like your food very hot then these aren't for you. The stuffing is very tasty, and if you're tempted to try it but daren't, try stuffing the mixture into small, scoop-shaped pieces of green pepper instead.

You can, if you're an absolute chilli addict, serve these just as a little snack on their own, but they're an excellent side dish with a selection of curries. Infused with mustard and asafoetida, they're particularly good with *dal* dishes.

....

12 fat, mild green chillies (Kenyan, Anaheim, jalapeño or poblano are good varieties to use)

FOR THE STUFFING

....

2 tablespoons *besan* (gram or chickpea flour)

$\frac{1}{2}$ teaspoon salt

$\frac{1}{8}$ teaspoon turmeric

$\frac{1}{8}$ teaspoon asafoetida

$\frac{1}{4}$ teaspoon *dhana jiru* (page 16)

$1\frac{1}{2}$ tablespoons groundnut (peanut) oil

2 teaspoons lemon juice

FOR THE VAGAR

....

1 tablespoon groundnut (peanut) oil

$\frac{1}{2}$ teaspoon mustard seeds

$\frac{1}{4}$ teaspoon cumin seeds

Pinch of fenugreek seeds

$\frac{1}{4}$ teaspoon asafoetida

Makes 12

....

Wash the chillies and dry them. Trim off any brown tips on the stems, then slit the chillies from stem to tip. If you want to remove the seeds, prise each chilli open carefully and scoop or cut away the seeds and the pale membrane that attaches them to the shell of the chilli.

Mix the ingredients for the stuffing together to make a thick, kneadable paste. Prise open the chillies and press the stuffing inside (see picture on page 137). Don't pack them too tight – if they're overfilled they might break open.

When the chillies are all stuffed, make the *vagar*. Put the oil in a large frying pan (skillet) – or any wide pan that has a lid – and warm over medium heat. Add the seeds and the asafoetida and cook for a few moments before adding the stuffed chillies. Stir gently to coat them with the spiced oil, then cover and cook until the chillies are soft, turning from time to time to ensure they cook evenly.

»*see pictures on the following pages*

Hot vegetable relish
Sambharo

Rose often makes this colourful mixture of lightly cooked vegetables spiked with chilli and curry leaves when she's cooking food for lots of people: it allows those who prefer hot food to add some fire to milder, crowd-friendly curries.

....

½ large hard white cabbage

3 medium-sized carrots

8 green chillies

2 tablespoons groundnut (peanut) oil

1 tablespoon mustard seeds

½ teaspoon asafoetida

2 branches of curry leaves (about 20 leaves)

⅛ teaspoon turmeric

2 teaspoons salt

Juice of 1 lemon

Enough for 10–15 people as an accompaniment

....

Cut the core from the cabbage and discard. Cut the leaves into 1cm-/½in-thick slices. Peel the carrots and cut into 5cm-/2in-long batons. Split the chillies from stem to tip and, if they are long, cut into 5cm/2in lengths.

Put the oil in a large, heavy-based pan over medium heat. Add the mustard seeds, asafoetida and curry leaves. As soon as they begin to sizzle, add the vegetables. Turn to coat with the oil, then add the turmeric, salt and lemon juice. Cover and cook for 10 minutes. Remove the lid to allow excess moisture to evaporate, and cook until the vegetables are tender but retaining some bite. Serve hot or cold. *Sambharo* will keep in the fridge for up to 2 weeks.

Chunky cucumber and tomato relish
Kachumber

Kachumber is always served with *akhni*, peas pilau and *biriani*: chilli-spiked lemon and crunchy vegetables add contrast to many dishes.

....

2 medium-sized red onions

2 firm tomatoes

10cm/4in section of cucumber

1 green chilli

½ teaspoon salt

Juice of 1 lemon

½ tablespoon chopped coriander (cilantro)

For 4 as an accompaniment

....

Quarter the onions and slice them thickly. Cut the tomatoes into large dice or thick slices. Halve the cucumber along its length and scoop out the seeds. Cut into large dice or thick half-moons. Cut the chilli into slim rounds.

Put the chopped vegetables into a non-reactive bowl. Sprinkle with the salt, then pour over the lemon juice. Toss well, then add the coriander and toss briefly again. Serve immediately.

Snacks, savouries and drinks

The recipes in this, the longest chapter of the book, are much loved, varied and versatile. They can be served at any time of day for a between-meal snack or light meal. Some, like *chilla* or *bhajia*, make a good breakfast; others, such as *samosa* or *chops*, are perfect for lunchboxes. Snacks and savouries, or *nasto*, are traditionally served in the afternoon with tea as a kind of pre-evening refresher. Guests calling mid morning or mid afternoon who can't be coaxed into staying for a meal will be offered one or two of the *nasto* in this chapter as a natural part of Indian hospitality. You could make a selection of these snacks and serve them in small portions for a drinks party. Or, if you want to follow Western protocol and serve an appetiser as part of your Indian meal, any of these dishes, served in suitably dainty portions, would work well. But why wait for a special occasion? Next time you feel a bit peckish, rustle up one of these tasty snacks – but let me warn you: they're highly addictive!

A GOOD CUP OF TEA is the best accompaniment to a plateful of any of the snacks in this chapter. You could serve a special milky, sweetly spiced *chai* (page 173), or just make a pot of good loose-leaf tea. Indian varieties work well – Assam or Ceylon would be good choices – or try a good-quality English Breakfast blend. Always use freshly boiled water, in a teapot if you have one, and brew the tea well: its full flavour will complement your snack perfectly.

Mixed vegetable fritters
Bhajia

These delicious fritters, made with vegetables dipped in a lightly spiced chickpea-flour batter, are the Gujarati version of *pakoras*. They can be made with all kinds of vegetables, whole chillies (if you can stand the heat) or, for an East African twist, bananas. Certain vegetables work particularly well, such as the ones I've suggested below. *Bhajia* are best eaten just after they're cooked, served with Tomato and Chilli Chutney (page 130), Tamarind Chutney (page 133), or Coriander Chutney (page 132).

3 cloves garlic (optional)

6cm/3in ginger

3 green chillies, topped and tailed

1 teaspoon cumin seeds

1 heaped teaspoon salt

40g/1½oz/¼ cup semolina

350g/12oz/3 cups *besan* (gram or chickpea flour)

3 tablespoons chopped coriander (cilantro)

1 head of broccoli, about 250g/9oz in weight

1 large red pepper

1 large red onion

1 baby or ½ medium aubergine (eggplant)

1 medium potato, peeled

Groundnut (peanut) oil for deep-frying

½ teaspoon baking powder or ¼ teaspoon bicarbonate of soda (baking soda)

Enough for 4 as a snack

Crush the garlic (if you are using it – sometimes Rose leaves it out for a cleaner flavour), ginger, chillies, cumin seeds and salt using a pestle and mortar, or whizz in a blender. Combine the semolina and *besan* in a large bowl and gradually beat in 250ml/8fl oz/1 cup of water. Add the ginger paste and coriander and set the batter aside while you prepare the vegetables.

Cut the broccoli into small florets, about 3cm/1¼in across, and discard the tough stem parts. (Any small leaves can be finely chopped and added to the batter.) Halve the pepper and remove the stem, seeds and white membranes inside. Cut each half lengthwise into 4 pieces. Cut the onion into 5mm/¼in rounds. Slice the aubergine as you did the onion, cutting off and discarding the stem and sepals first. Peel the potato and cut into 3mm/⅛in slices.

Next, heat the oil for frying. If you are using a wok or *karai*, fill it to a third of its depth with oil and heat over a medium flame. When the oil is only just warm, remove a quarter of a ladleful of it and stir this into the batter. Wait for the oil to reach frying temperature – test by adding a drop of batter to the oil. If it rises to the top, coated in bubbles, then the oil is ready for frying. (If you are using a deep-fat fryer, set the thermostat to 170°C/340°F.)

When the oil in the pan is up to frying temperature, add the bicarbonate of soda or baking powder to the batter and mix thoroughly. Add a little water if necessary – it should have the consistency of cake batter or thick custard.

Next, working fairly quickly now, drop the vegetable pieces into the batter. Mix them around a bit, then remove them (they should　»

» be coated thickly with batter) and lower them carefully into the oil. At first, fry only a couple of pieces until they are crisp and golden-brown. This should take 5–10 minutes, depending on their size. Remove them with a slotted spoon and sit them on some kitchen paper to allow excess oil to drain away. When they are cool enough, taste them to see if your batter needs some more salt. Adjust the seasoning in the mixture accordingly and proceed.

Cook the *bhajia* in small batches – you'll probably manage about 6 in the pan at once. Stir gently from time to time to ensure they cook evenly. Once they are done, drain thoroughly on kitchen paper. Serve the *bhajia* with the chutneys and some fruit juice or tea.

Some variations

Cabbage, spinach or fenugreek leaves can be added to the above vegetables.

Whole chillies, if you're a chilli addict, are delicious simply dipped in the batter and fried on their own. Nibble on one of these, if you dare, between other *bhajia*.

Bananas are an interesting sweet surprise in a plateful of otherwise savoury *bhajia*. Peel a couple of (preferably slightly underripe) bananas and cut into 2cm/¾in chunks. Dip into the batter to coat quite thickly and fry as above.

Cauliflower, carrot and courgette (zucchini) are other great additions. Prepare the cauliflower as per the broccoli; cut the carrot and courgettes in 5mm/¼in diagonal slices.

Corn with pepper butter
Tareli makai

The usual spices don't appear in this simple side dish: black pepper alone adds fragrance and heat. Use the freshest corn you can find – buy it in its leafy sheath, which should look fresh and green – because the flavour of corn deteriorates rapidly from the moment it is picked.

2 cobs (ears) fresh corn, husks and silks removed
25g/1oz/2 tablespoons butter
½ teaspoon salt
¾ teaspoon freshly ground black pepper

For 2 as a side dish or snack with chappatis

Slice the kernels from the corn cobs. Melt the butter is a small frying pan (skillet) over medium heat, then add the corn. Sprinkle with the salt and stir-fry. When the corn begins to soften, add half of the black pepper.

Continue to cook until the corn begins to turn a toasty golden-brown. Add the remaining pepper and serve hot.

Cassava chips
Tarelo mogo

Rose first made these chunky chips for me after a winter's morning trawling the local markets for ingredients when we began gathering recipes for this book. My stomach was rumbling and I was beginning to get grumpy, but Rose tried to cheer me up with the promise of a plate of *mogo* when we got home. I'd never eaten cassava before, but I saw the strange root in Rose's bag and was unimpressed. Later, however, with a plate of cassava chips in front of me, grumpiness was supplanted by greed, and I was again a happy man. With their crunchy crusts and fluffy centres, sprinkled with chilli and salt, then dipped in tamarind chutney, fried cassava chips make a brilliant snack. I polished off my share, then some of everyone else's ...

Cassava looks like a section of tree branch, with a bark-like skin and a diameter of about 15cm/6in. You may be lucky enough to find it in your local supermarket – if not, try an Indian, Chinese, Caribbean or African grocer's (*mogo* is the Swahili name). Fresh cassava is easily prepared – but frozen packets of peeled and parboiled roots are even more convenient. If you can find them in this form, buy them: cassava can be cooked quickly from frozen; with a pack in the freezer, you'll always have a moreishly tasty snack on standby.

750g/1lb 10oz fresh cassava root, peeled, or half a 900g/2lb pack of frozen cassava
Groundnut (peanut) oil for deep-frying
Chilli powder for sprinkling
Salt for sprinkling

Enough for 2 greedy people as a snack

If you're using fresh cassava, cut it into 8cm-/3in-long pieces. Put the cassava pieces – frozen or fresh – in a large pan and cover with water. Bring to the boil and cook until tender. With fresh, this may take up to 40 minutes, but frozen will take something more like 20 minutes. But beware: all of the cassava pieces will not take the same amount of time to cook, so check each periodically with a sharp knife. You'll find they often split open once they're cooked.

As soon as each piece of *mogo* is ready, hoist it out with a slotted spoon onto a chopping board. When the roots are cool enough to handle, split them open along their length with a knife and cut them into wedge-shaped chips. Discard any wiry or woody fibres running down the centres of the roots.

Get the oil ready for frying. If you are using a wok or *karai*, fill it to a third of its depth with oil and heat over a medium flame. Test whether the oil is up to frying temperature by dropping a piece of *mogo* into it – if the chip rises to the top immediately and is coated in bubbles, then the oil is ready. If you are using a deep-fat fryer, set the thermostat to 170°C/340°F.

Fry the chips in batches, then drain on kitchen paper. Sprinkle with chilli and salt, and serve hot with Tamarind Chutney (page 133).

Spicy snack mix
Chevro

We've included this, the Gujarati version of the ubiquitous Bombay Mix, despite the fact that one or two ingredients may be tricky to find and it is quite labour-intensive, just because it's so delicious. Forget overspiced, greasy, often stale store-bought Bombay Mix – this is light, crispy and irresistibly spicy.

Usually made in enormous quantities for special occasions, this recipe is a throwback to times when several generations of women in large extended families would cook together in preparation for weddings and feast days. There are many separate stages – you can imagine one lady frying crisps (potato chips) while another prepares peanuts, with the matriarch mixing and spicing it all as each component is cooked.

While testing this recipe for the book, Rose told me about a 'tip' she was given for drying large quantities of the soaked chickpeas: one of Rose's friends told her she drains her chickpeas, pops them into a clean pillowcase, and then into her washing machine for a spin cycle! (We haven't tried this – and we don't recommend it!)

You won't need to employ such quasi-mass-production techniques: preparing a smaller quantity makes this recipe manageable for one or two people. Why not spend a rainy afternoon in the kitchen with the radio on (preferably tuned to Sunrise Radio, with their playlist of old Bollywood tunes) and make yourself a stash of this tasty snack? *Chevro* keeps well for a couple of months if stored in an airtight container.

Makes about 900g/2lb

Groundnut (peanut) oil for deep-frying

450g/1lb *channa dal* (split chickpeas) soaked overnight, then drained and dried in a salad spinner

1.35kg/3lb potatoes, peeled and grated

550g/1¼lb potatoes, peeled and shaved into crisps with a food processor or mandoline

225g/8oz/2 cups peanuts

110g/4oz/1 cup cashew nuts

Handful of sultanas (golden raisins)

5 green chillies, cut into 5mm/¼in pieces

1 double-handful of coriander (cilantro) leaves, washed and dried in a salad spinner

225g/8oz flaked rice (*pawa*)

FOR THE VAGAR

3 tablespoons groundnut (peanut) oil

1 large, dried red Kashmiri chilli, broken into 4

About 20 curry leaves

2 tablespoons fennel seeds

3 tablespoons sesame seeds

3 teaspoons mustard seeds

8 cloves

1 heaped teaspoon asafoetida

TO FINISH

1–1½ teaspoons chilli powder to taste

½ teaspoon turmeric

2 teaspoons caster (superfine) sugar

1½ teaspoons salt

Fill a large wok or *karai* to a third of its depth with oil and place over medium-high heat. Have ready several plates lined with kitchen paper. Drop a piece of *channa dal* into the oil and, »

» when it floats, you are ready to fry. (Regulate the heat as you cook to keep the temperature as even as possible: increase the heat a little when you add anything to the oil and reduce it slightly once frying steadily.)

In small batches of a large spoonful or so at a time, fry the *channa dal*. They should take a few minutes to become crispy and pale, and to float. Drain the chickpeas and remove them to a paper-lined plate. Discard any pieces of *dal* that refuse to float.

Put the grated potato into a clean tea towel, wrap tightly and then, over the sink, wring the cloth to squeeze any excess moisture out of the potato. Remove from the cloth and separate the shreds with your fingers. Fry the grated potato in batches until golden-brown, then drain on kitchen paper. As the cooked batches cool, tip them into your largest heatproof mixing bowl (or a large saucepan). It is very important that the *chevro* is kept as dry as possible, so make sure everything is well drained and blotted free of oil before it is put into the mixing bowl.

Next, fry the potato slices in small batches until golden-brown. Drain them on kitchen paper.

Reduce the heat slightly and then fry the peanuts until they begin to pop. Remove them and drain on kitchen paper. Next, fry the cashew nuts until they are pale gold and drain on paper.

Increase the heat and fry the sultanas until crispy, removing them to kitchen paper to drain as you go. Do the same with the chillies (you'll need to open a window and put on your extractor as they give off pungent fumes!) and the coriander leaves.

Finally, fry the flaked rice: cook in small batches and stand by – it will puff up quickly. Once puffed, remove it immediately. Don't let it brown at all – it should remain pale.

Once everything has been drained, blotted, cooled and well mixed in the bowl, make the *vagar*. Heat the oil in a frying pan (skillet) until hot, add the red chilli and, when it blackens, add the curry leaves, the fennel, sesame and mustard seeds, the cloves and asafoetida. When the curry leaves are crisp, tip the spiced oil over the *chevro*. Take a metal spoon and give everything a good stir. Sprinkle with the chilli powder, turmeric, sugar and salt. Mix well, then taste and adjust the seasonings as you wish.

Allow the mixture to cool completely before packing into airtight containers which you have lined with sheets of kitchen paper, to help keep the mixture dry.

MAKE SURE you follow the specific running order given in the method for frying the *chevro* ingredients. Some components, such as the chillies and *pawa*, taint the oil, so they're fried at the end. *Channa dal* and potatoes are absorbent so, to preserve their particular flavours, they are fried first.

Chickpeas and potatoes with tamarind
Channa bateta

Tangy and spicy, this is a typical Gujarati street snack, sold from stalls in bustling market streets. My wife's cousin Sheila tells me that, when she was growing up in the township of Mwanza in Tanzania, *channa bateta* was served at every birthday party she went to. Traditionally topped with a sprinkling of *chevro*, sliced onions and coriander (cilantro), it's a lively mix of textures and flavours. If you've taken the time to make our *Chevro* recipe (page 147), go the extra mile and make this special classic accompaniment.

2 large waxy (round white or round red) potatoes, peeled and cut into 2cm/¾in dice

2 tablespoons groundnut (peanut) oil

1 dried red Kashmiri chilli

½ teaspoon mustard seeds

½ teaspoon cumin seeds

½ teaspoon asafoetida

10 curry leaves

200ml/7fl oz crushed canned plum tomatoes and juice (about half a can)

½ teaspoon chilli powder

½ teaspoon turmeric

1¼ teaspoons salt

2 x 400g/14oz cans chickpeas, drained and thoroughly rinsed

1 tablespoon *besan* (gram or chickpea flour)

125ml/4fl oz/½ cup tamarind water, prepared as on page 133 (or 1 teaspoon tamarind concentrate blended with 125ml/4fl oz/½ cup hot water)

1 tablespoon chopped coriander (cilantro) leaves

Serves 6 as a snack

Put the potatoes in a pan of cold water and bring to the boil. Simmer for 5 minutes, then drain and set aside.

Put the oil in a large pan over medium heat and add the red chilli. As it darkens, add the mustard seeds, cumin seeds, asafoetida and curry leaves. After a few seconds only, add the tomatoes, chilli powder, turmeric and salt. Bring to a boil, then simmer rapidly until the oil pools around the sides of the pan. Add the chickpeas and potatoes and stir to coat with the *masala*.

Mix the *besan* to a smooth cream with 625ml/22fl oz/2½ cups of water and stir this into the *masala*. Continue to stir as you bring the *masala* to the boil, then add the tamarind water. Simmer for 10–15 minutes more until thickened, then serve in small bowls, sprinkled with the chopped coriander leaves. Or, if you have some *chevro*, sprinkle a little on each serving of *channa bateta* and top with sliced red onions and the chopped coriander leaves.

Steamed savoury cake
Dhokra

Typically Gujarati, these spongy squares have an unusual, mildly sour flavour. I must admit, when I discovered Eno's Fruit Salt was one of the ingredients I was spooked – it seemed so un-foodish (it's an antacid, available from chemists or drugstores). But in fact it's only a mix of citric acid (lemon juice), bicarbonate of soda (baking soda) and cream of tartar – all common cooking ingredients – and it aerates the batter so effectively that I've given up looking for less weird-sounding alternatives.

Rose has special *dhokra*-making equipment, but you can improvise. You'll need two shallow 25cm/10in cake pans, a saucepan (with a lid) wide enough to hold one pan, and a trivet to support the pan inside the saucepan.

Serve with Tomato and Chilli Chutney (page 130) or Coriander Chutney (page 132).

4 cloves garlic

4cm/1½in ginger

3 green chillies

½ teaspoon cumin seeds

2 teaspoons salt

500g/1lb 2oz/3 cups fine semolina

1 tablespoon *besan* (gram or chickpea flour)

325ml/12fl oz/1½ cups yoghurt

¼ teaspoon turmeric

2½ tablespoons groundnut (peanut) oil

½ teaspoon citric acid

½ teaspoon bicarbonate of soda (baking soda)

2 tablespoons chopped coriander (cilantro)

2 heaped teaspoons Eno's Fruit Salt (see above)

Chilli powder for sprinkling

Makes 2 25cm/10in cakes

Pound the garlic, ginger, chillies, cumin seeds and salt to a paste. In a bowl, combine the semolina, *besan*, yoghurt, turmeric, oil, citric acid, bicarbonate of soda, coriander and the garlic-ginger paste. Mix well to a stiff paste.

Put the trivet into the saucepan. Pour in enough water to come halfway up the trivet. Cover with the saucepan lid wrapped in a tea towel (to stop condensation dripping onto the cake). Put the pan on the heat and bring to the boil. Oil the cake pans and put one inside the saucepan to heat up (see picture on page 152, bottom left).

Divide the paste into two equal portions, setting one aside in a separate bowl. To the first portion of paste, add 250ml/8fl oz/1 cup of boiling water to make a fairly thick batter. Working quickly, add half the Eno's and mix well, then remove the lid from the saucepan and pour the batter into the preheated cake pan. Sprinkle with a pinch of chilli powder and cover with the lid.

Steam for 20 minutes until the cake is springy and not sticky when pressed. Remove the cake pan to a cooling rack and put the other cake pan inside the steamer pan to preheat. Mix and cook the second batch of batter as you did the first (you may need to add a little more water this time – a couple of tablespoons or so – as the mixture has stood a little longer). When the cakes have cooled a little, cut into 10cm/4in squares. Serve, preferably warm, with chutney.

» *see pictures on the following pages*

Vegetable cake
Hondwo

Rose's mother learned the recipe for this savoury Gujarati teatime snack from a neighbouring Hindu family in their village in Uganda – so this recipe includes asafoetida (which is usually absent in *Khoja* versions of *hondwo*). It's one of those dishes that would have been rustled up by a crack team of female relatives in the kitchen together, but don't be put off. It's well worth the effort – one cake will give at least ten good-sized servings – and, although the ingredients list is long, most items will be in your kitchen cupboard already. *Hondwo* has a subtle, mildly sour flavour that's somehow addictive. When preparing this book, we tested the recipe several times – perhaps more than strictly necessary!

Try this unusual snack out on your friends – or better still, get them roped into cooking it with you. Serve your *hondwo* cut into wedges to reveal the colourful mosaic of vegetables inside, with Masala Tea (page 173) and any chutney. Green Mango and Coriander Chutney (page 132) is a particularly good accompaniment.

Oil for greasing
375g/14oz/2 cups coarse semolina
120g/4oz/1 cup *besan* (gram or chickpea flour)
350ml/12fl oz/1½ cups yoghurt
125ml/4fl oz/½ cup groundnut (peanut) oil
2 fat cloves garlic
8cm/3in ginger
5 green chillies
1 teaspoon cumin seeds
1 large carrot
2 medium onions

1 small potato
¼ red pepper
15cm/6in section of bottle gourd (*dudhi*)
¼ hard white cabbage, core removed
3 spring onions (scallions)
3 tablespoons chopped coriander (cilantro) leaves, plus a tablespoon of finely chopped stems
1 tablespoon chopped fenugreek leaves
50g/2oz/½ cup frozen peas
2 teaspoons sugar
Juice of 1 lemon
2 teaspoons salt

FOR THE VAGAR

125ml/4fl oz/½ cup groundnut (peanut) oil
2 teaspoons mustard seeds
½ teaspoon cumin seeds
12 curry leaves
Generous ½ teaspoon asafoetida

TO FINISH

2½ teaspoon Eno's Fruit Salt (see page 151)
Large pinch of mustard seeds
1 tablespoon sesame seeds
Curry leaves to decorate

Makes 1 23cm/9in cake

Oil a 23cm/9in springform cake pan and preheat the oven to 210°C/410°F/gas mark 7. Mix the semolina, *besan*, yoghurt and oil in a bowl and set aside while you prepare the vegetables. Pound the garlic, ginger, chillies and cumin seeds to a paste. Peel the carrot, »

» onions and potato, and dice them finely along with the red pepper. Peel the bottle gourd and grate it coarsely. Finely shred the cabbage and finely slice the spring onions.

Once all the vegetables are ready, add them to the batter with the garlic-ginger paste, coriander leaves and stems, fenugreek leaves, peas, sugar, lemon juice and salt. Mix well with your hands (the dough will be quite stiff).

Next, make the *vagar*. Heat the oil in a frying pan (skillet). When hot, add the mustard and cumin seeds – they will pop, so have a lid handy to cover the pan. Add the curry leaves and the asafoetida, cook for just a few seconds, then tip this over the batter mixture in the bowl.

Add 60ml/2fl oz/¼ cup of hot water and mix thoroughly with a wooden spoon. To finish, add the Eno's and, working quickly, mix again and pour into the prepared cake pan. Level the top with a knife, sprinkle with the mustard and sesame seeds and decorate with a few curry leaves. Place in the centre of the oven and cook for 15 minutes, then reduce the temperature to 190°C/375°F/gas mark 5. Cook for a further 1–1½ hours until the cake is springy when pressed and has turned a burnished dark-brown colour. Remove from the oven and cool in the pan for about 30 minutes (if you try to cut it straight from the oven you will find the middle soft and sticky). Take the cake out of the pan, put it on a plate and cut into slices. Serve warm or cold, with chutney.

Grilled corn with chilli and lime
Sekeli makai

More of a serving suggestion than a recipe, this toothsome snack is excellent with barbecue food. Rose is very fond of corn on the cob; it takes her back to childhood days in Uganda when she and her siblings would steal ears of corn from the fields near their home and eat them, raw, tender and juicily sweet, hiding amongst the tall maize.

FOR EACH PERSON

1 cob (ear) fresh corn, husk and silks removed
1 lime wedge
Chilli powder to taste
Salt to taste

Preheat your overhead grill (broiler) to a medium-high setting (or, if you are going to barbecue the corn, wait until the coals are glowing under a layer of greyish-white ash).

Put the corn fairly close to the heat and grill without turning until the kernels become a honeyed golden-brown. Rotate the corn to expose the next section of uncooked cob to the heat and cook until browned. Work your way around the corn until it is golden-brown all over.

To eat, put the corn on your plate and squeeze over the lime. Sprinkle with chilli powder and salt, and get nibbling – have napkins handy!

Spring onion and chilli pancakes
Chilla

Although these are technically pancakes, *chilla* are really more like omelettes – light yet filling, and very easy to make. They're a great snack to share with unexpected guests (most of the ingredients are from the storecupboard), or you could serve them for brunch with Masala Tea (page 173) and perhaps some papaya halves with fresh lime squeezed over to follow.

Serve *chilla* with any of the chutneys on pages 130–133 – all work well.

2 fat cloves garlic

2.5cm/1in ginger

1 green chilli, roughly chopped

1 teaspoon salt

6 tablespoons *besan* (gram or chickpea flour)

1 tablespoon plain (all-purpose) flour

1 egg, beaten

2 spring onions (scallions), chopped

1½ tablespoons chopped coriander (cilantro) leaves

Groundnut (peanut) oil for frying

Makes 6 *chilla*

Crush the garlic, ginger, chilli and salt to a paste. Sift the *besan* and plain flour into a mixing bowl. Make a well in the centre and add the egg, spring onions and coriander and mix thoroughly until evenly blended. Add about 300ml/10fl oz/1¼ cups water to make a batter the consistency of single (light) cream. Set a small pot of oil and a pastry brush at the side of the stove.

Coat the base of a (preferably non-stick) frying pan (skillet) with a thin film of oil and set over a medium heat. Take a ladleful of batter and pour in just enough batter to cover the base of the pan, swirling it around to coat the base evenly (an average ladleful is just about right for a 20cm/8in omelette pan).

Cook on a medium heat until the top has set entirely and the edges are browning lacily. Brush the top of the pancake very lightly with oil, then loosen the *chilla* with a palette knife (metal spatula) and flip over. (As with all pancakes, you'll probably find that the first one is a bit of a mess, but after that you'll have got the heat right and things will go much better.) Cook until the *chilla* is patched golden-brown, then remove to a warm plate.

Proceed with the rest of the batter in this way, sparingly oiling the pan as you need to. Stack the pancakes on the plate as you go, to keep warm until you're ready to eat.

Potato croquettes with peas
Mattar na chops

If it wasn't for these spicy, zesty little potato cakes filled with a heavenly mixture of spiced peas and onions, this book may never have happened. My wife, Salima, and I first met at work: we became friends and, during lunchbreaks, would often decamp to the local park where we'd share our home-cooked lunches. At that time, Salima was living with her parents and Rose, in typical Indian-mother style, would fill Salima's lunchboxes with the most delicious little morsels. These chops were the first thing that I tasted; I was instantly captivated by their subtle flavour – and by the woman who was sweet enough to share them with me.

Remarkably, the fresh, lively flavour of the chops comes from earthy dried green peas, enlivened with chillies, onions, lemon, coriander (cilantro) and *garam masala*. Have lemon wedges to squeeze over, or some Tomato and Chilli Chutney (page 130) or Coriander Chutney (page 132) to dip them into – and, please, try not to scoff the whole batch yourself!

FOR THE FILLING

225g/8oz/1 cup dried whole green peas, soaked for at least 24 hours

4 green chillies, stems removed

6 cloves garlic

5cm/2in ginger

1½ teaspoons salt

3 medium onions, very finely chopped

Groundnut (peanut) oil for frying

4 tablespoons finely chopped (cilantro) coriander

¼ teaspoon *garam masala* (page 16)

TO MAKE UP

900g/2lb floury (long white or russet) potatoes, peeled

Juice of half a lemon

1 teaspoon salt

110g/4oz/½ cup semolina

2 eggs

Makes 25 croquettes

Drain and rinse the dried peas, then blitz them in a food processor with the green chillies until they're finely chopped. Pound the garlic, ginger and 1 teaspoon of the salt to a paste, then add it to the peas with a third of the chopped onions.

Put 3 tablespoons of oil in a wide, preferably non-stick, frying pan (skillet) and set over medium heat. Add the pea mixture and stir-fry until dry and no longer sticking together. Stir in the *garam masala* and ½ teaspoon of salt and set the pea mixture aside to cool completely.

Meanwhile, put the potatoes in a pan and cover them with water. Bring up to the boil and simmer for 20 minutes or so until tender. Drain the potatoes in a colander, then mash them thoroughly until smooth. Add the lemon juice and 1 teaspoon of salt and allow to cool a little.

When the pea mixture is absolutely cold, add the remaining chopped onions and the chopped coriander. Stir the pea mixture into the potatoes, mix well, then shape into sausage-like cylinders, about 8cm/3in long and 3cm/1¼in wide.   »

» Fill a small bowl with water and set it beside a plate spread with the semolina. Line a baking sheet (cookie sheet) with greaseproof (waxed) paper. Dip each croquette briefly into the water, then roll in the semolina to coat lightly. Brush off any excess semolina and set the croquettes on the paper-lined tray as you proceed.

Beat the eggs with 2 tablespoons of water in a shallow bowl and place near the stove. Set a large deep pan, wok or *karai* over medium heat and fill it to a third of its depth with oil. (If you're using a deep-fat fryer with a thermostat, set it to 160°C/325°F.) To test if the oil is up to frying temperature, drop a small piece of bread into the pan. If it bubbles gently and rises to the surface, you're ready to fry.

When ready to fry, dip a croquette into the egg, wait a second to allow any excess egg to drain off, then add the croquette to the hot oil. Repeat with more croquettes until you have a small batch cooking – don't overcrowd the pan, or the temperature of the oil will drop. Gently turn the chops frequently to brown them evenly then, when they are brown all over, reduce the heat slightly and cook for a few minutes more. Remove the croquettes and drain them on kitchen paper. Repeat the process until all the chops are cooked. Serve hot, warm or cold, with chutney and lemon wedges.

Lamb filling for potato croquettes
Ghosh no kheemo

For this equally tasty variation of the previous recipe, follow the above method but substitute the pea filling for the lamb version given here.

350g/12oz lean minced (ground) lamb
4 cloves garlic
4cm/1½in ginger
4 green chillies, trimmed and thickly sliced
1 teaspoon salt
½ teaspoon *garam masala* (page 16)
2 medium onions, very finely chopped
1 tablespoon finely chopped coriander (cilantro) stems
1 tablespoon finely chopped coriander (cilantro) leaves

Dry-fry the meat over high heat until it is light brown and almost all of the juices exuded from the meat have evaporated. Pound the garlic, ginger, chillies and salt to a paste. Add to the lamb and reduce the heat to medium. Cook until the meat is dry and beginning to stick to the pan. Add the *garam masala*, then turn off the heat and leave to cool. When completely cold, add the onions and chopped coriander stems and leaves.

Follow the instructions in the preceding recipe for the preparation of the potatoes, assembling of the croquettes and the deep-frying.

Lamb patties
Cutlets

Juicy and moreish, these Indian-style burgers are an excellent snack, stuffed into pittas with lettuce, *Raitha* (page 130) and Coriander Chutney (page 132). Rose was never very fond of this dish and seldom cooked it until fairly recently when she was helping to make food for her niece's wedding. Rose and her sister-in-law's sister Anar made 350 of these for the celebration feast, to Anar's own recipe, and it was the subtlest of things – the inclusion of mint – that perked up Rose's interest in the dish.

Normally, these are lightly cooked, then coated in egg and fried. Rose feels frying isn't necessary, so has adapted Anar's recipe to omit this step and employ the healthier method of cooking in the oven.

Organic meat will serve you best – it won't shrink or exude any juices, and so the patties will be less likely to break in the cooking.

Groundnut (peanut) oil for greasing

900g/2lb lean minced (ground) lamb

4 cloves garlic

4cm/1$\frac{1}{2}$in ginger

3 green chillies, trimmed and thickly sliced

1$\frac{1}{2}$ teaspoons salt

1 slice white bread

1 small onion, grated

1 tablespoon finely chopped mint leaves

2 tablespoons finely chopped coriander (cilantro) leaves

$\frac{1}{2}$ teaspoon *garam masala* (page 16)

Makes 10 patties, enough for 4 greedy people

Lightly oil 2 baking trays (pans) and preheat your oven to 220°C/425°F/gas mark 7.

Put the lamb in a large bowl. Pound the garlic, ginger, chillies and salt to a paste and add it to the lamb. Soak the bread in cold water for a few moments, then squeeze it out and add it to the lamb with the remaining ingredients. Mix thoroughly with your hands, then divide the mixture into 10 compact balls. Flatten the balls into 10cm/4in rounds (you'll find it easier to shape neat patties if your hands are oiled) and arrange them on the baking sheets.

Bake the patties for 10 minutes until they have 'set' – they won't have browned at all, but they will have become quite firm. Turn a patty over – if it breaks, return the patties to the oven, without turning, for another 5 minutes. Then flip all the patties and cook for 10 minutes more. Serve hot.

Vegetable samosas
Bhoga na samosa

Once you've eaten homemade samosas, served fresh and crisp from a *karai* of crackling hot oil with a squeeze of lemon, you'll never want to touch stodgy, greasy store-bought ones again. Rose's recipe has a wonderfully light, fresh flavour that's beautifully complemented by her delicate, crisp homemade *pur* (pastry). Although making samosas at home involves a little work, folding and filling them is fun.

1½ tablespoons groundnut (peanut) oil

1 dried red Kashmiri chilli

½ teaspoon mustard seeds

¼ teaspoon cumin seeds

Pinch of fenugreek seeds

Scant ½ teaspoon asafoetida

10 curry leaves

¼ teaspoon turmeric

2 large carrots, peeled and finely diced

3 small potatoes, peeled and finely diced

1 clove garlic

4cm/1½in ginger

¾ teaspoon salt

¼ green cabbage, cored and finely chopped

110g/4oz/1 cup frozen peas

1 tablespoon lemon juice

2 green chillies, trimmed and finely chopped

½ teaspoon caster (superfine) sugar

½ teaspoon *samosa masala* (page 17)

1 small onion, very finely chopped

4 spring onions (scallions), very finely chopped (green and white parts)

1 tablespoon finely chopped coriander (cilantro) leaves

Pinch of *garam masala* (page 16)

TO MAKE UP

3 tablespoons strong white bread flour

1 quantity Samosa Pastry (page 167), or 20 ready-made wrappers

Groundnut (peanut) oil for deep-frying

Makes 20

Put the oil in a large pan and, over medium heat, add the red chilli. As soon as the chilli begins to darken, add the mustard, cumin and fenugreek seeds, the asafoetida, curry leaves and turmeric. Cook the spices for a few seconds only, then add the carrots and stir well to coat with the spice-infused oil.

Cover the pan and reduce the heat to medium-low. Cook the carrots for 5 minutes, then add the potatoes. Stir well, cover and cook for 5 minutes more. Meanwhile, pound the garlic, ginger and salt to a paste and set aside.

When the potatoes have had their 5 minutes, add the cabbage, peas, lemon juice, garlic-ginger paste, chillies and sugar. Reduce the heat to low and cook, stirring from time to time, for 10 minutes, until the vegetables are tender, but retaining some bite. Remove from the heat, add the *samosa masala* and leave to cool completely.

When the vegetables are cold, mix in the onion, spring onions, coriander and *garam masala*.

To make up the samosas, mix the flour with 1 tablespoon of cold water to make a thick, smooth paste. You'll need this paste to seal each »

» of the samosas once they are folded and stuffed. Follow the instructions and diagrams below for folding the pastry and filling.

Next, heat the oil for frying. If you are using a wok or *karai*, fill it to a third of its depth with oil and heat over a medium flame. To find out if it's up to frying temperature, drop a small piece of

bread into the oil – if it rises to the top, coated in bubbles, the oil is ready. If you are using a deep-fat fryer, set the thermostat to 160°C/325°F.

Fry the samosas in small batches, turning often until evenly browned. Drain well and sit them on a plate lined with kitchen paper to absorb excess oil. Serve hot or cold.

How to fold and fill samosas

Having made your *pur* (pastry) following the recipe on page 167, you'll have cut your rounds of pastry to end up with trapezium shapes (see opposite, top left). Take one of these shapes and lay it across the palm of your hand so your view of it is the same as shown in diagram **1**, below. Fold across the dotted line: this fold doesn't need to be parallel to the edge of the dough – it's more important that it's at the correct angle to form the side of a roughly equilateral triangle (indicated in pink) – the finished shape of your samosa. Next, fold across the dotted line as shown in diagram **2**. You have now created a pocket – see diagram **3** (and opposite, top right). To fill, rotate the pocket so that it's positioned as shown in diagram **4**. Insert the filling using a spoon as directed (see

also opposite, bottom left). Don't overfill your pocket or it will be difficult to seal properly. When the pocket is nicely filled with your chosen filling, use some of the flour-and-water paste to coat the flaps thinly and evenly, as indicated in diagram **5** (see also opposite, bottom right), then fold along the indicated dotted line. Press the flaps down firmly to secure them. You should now have a neat triangular parcel, as shown in diagram **6**. Check all corners are sealed (if they're not, your samosa will fill with oil when it's frying). Apply a little paste and press the pastry together where necessary. Set your samosa on a plate while you make up the rest.

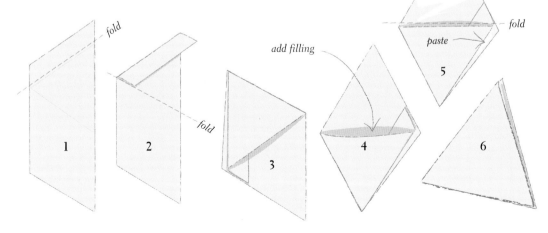

Lamb samosa filling
Ghosh no kheemo

These delicious, savoury morsels were a regular feature of my wife's school lunchboxes. But she rarely got to eat them because her friends would swarm her lunchbox to get hold of them!

450g/1lb lean minced (ground) lamb
4 cloves garlic
4cm/1½in ginger
3 green chillies, trimmed and thickly sliced
½ teaspoon salt
½ teaspoon *garam masala* (page 16)
2 small onions, very finely chopped
3 tablespoons finely chopped coriander (cilantro) leaves

To fill 20 wrappers

Follow the recipe for Vegetable Samosas (pages 163–164), substituting the filling with this mixture. Set a frying pan (skillet) over high heat. Dry-fry the lamb, stirring constantly to break up lumps. Cook until the meat is brown and only a little juice remains. Pound the garlic, ginger, chillies and salt to a paste and add to the lamb. Cook until dry (squeeze the meat against the side of the pan – if no juices run out, it's cooked). Stir in the *garam masala*, remove from the heat and cool completely. When the meat is absolutely cold, stir in the onions and coriander.

Chicken samosa filling
Kukra no kheemo

My favourite samosa filling – I like the lightness of the meat with the rich spicing.

450g/1lb minced (ground) chicken
4 cloves garlic
5cm/2in ginger
¼ fresh red chilli
½ teaspoon cumin seeds
1 teaspoon salt
1 teaspoon *garam masala* (page 16)
Juice of half a lemon
1 small onion, very finely chopped
4 spring onions (scallions), very finely chopped
3 tablespoons finely chopped coriander (cilantro)

To fill 20 wrappers

Follow the recipe for Vegetable Samosas (pages 163–164), substituting the filling with this mixture. Place a frying pan (skillet) over high heat and add the chicken. Dry-fry, stirring frequently to break up any lumps. Cook until the meat is white and only a little juice remains.

Pound the garlic, ginger, chilli, cumin and salt to a paste and add it to the chicken. Cook until the mixture is quite dry. Add the *garam masala* and lemon juice, remove from the heat and cool completely. When the meat is absolutely cold, stir in the onion, spring onions and coriander.

Samosa pastry
Samosa pur

If you live near an Indian grocer or supermarket, you'll probably have no problem finding ready-made samosa wrappers. Accept no substitutes – filo pastry or any other kind of dough just will not do! If you can't find ready-made, you can make them yourself. They're a little fiddly and time-consuming to make, but they are the real thing – and of course, better than anything you'll get in the shops.

225g/8oz/2 cups strong white bread flour, plus extra for dusting
¾ teaspoon salt
Groundnut oil for brushing

Makes 20 wrappers

Put the flour and salt in a bowl and add about 150ml/5fl oz/⅔ cup of cold water to make a stiff dough. Flour your surface, turn out the dough and knead for 5 minutes until stiff and elastic.

Divide the mixture into 10 equal-sized balls and flatten each one slightly. Flour your work surface and rolling pin, then roll the first ball into a 15cm/6in diameter round. Brush the top of the round with oil and dust lightly with flour. Roll the next 4 out to about 14cm/5½in and stack them in the centre of the first round, oiling and flouring each layer as you go and aligning them as carefully as you can.

Using your hands, press the stacked rounds all around the edge, squashing them slightly so that they spread to become the same diameter as the bottom round. Then turn the stack over and roll

with your rolling pin, as evenly as you can, to make a 23cm/9in round. Repeat the whole process to make another stack with the remaining 5 balls of dough.

Heat a *tava* or frying pan (skillet), large enough to take the dough round, on a low heat. Dampen a clean tea towel and keep it handy.

When the *tava* is thoroughly heated, place the first stack of dough on the pan and turn the heat to high. Cook briefly, rotating the dough from time to time, until the underside is pale and dry-looking – it should not brown. Turn the stack and cook the other side in this way. As soon as it is dry, remove the stack to a board and carefully peel apart the separate layers. As each of the layers is removed, re-stack them inside the damp tea towel, keeping them covered with the cloth as you work.

Cook and separate the second stack in the same way, stacking the peeled layers on top of the first batch. Make sure your stack is neatly aligned, then move it to a board. Take a sharp knife and cut right through the stack to make 2 equal semicircles. Then trim the edges as shown in the picture on page 165 (top left). (Any scraps can be discarded, or fried in hot oil, sprinkled with chilli powder and salt, and eaten as a snack.)

Keep wrapped in the tea towel until you are ready to use. Fold and fill as directed on page 164. These wrappers freeze well – cool them in the damp towel, wrap them in clingfilm (plastic wrap), then in foil, and place flat in the freezer. They can be defrosted overnight in the fridge.

Rose-flavoured milk shake
Sherbat

Baby-pink milk, laced with nuts, ice cream and fragrant, jelly-like *takmaria* (sweet basil) seeds: you're unlikely to find a crazier-looking drink – at least one made from such innocuous, relatively wholesome ingredients! Despite a rather unsubtle appearance, *sherbat* is very refreshing and has a delightful, creamy flavour, delicately perfumed with roses.

In the time of the Moghul emperors, ice cream was not used to cool this most aristocratic of refreshments: instead, snow from the Himalayas was sent for. Such lengths are not called for in this recipe, but I would urge you to use a good vanilla ice cream, made with real vanilla and full-cream (whole) milk. It will have a rich, mild flavour, in keeping with the other flavours here (cheap ice cream often tastes powdery and chemical). You should be able to find rose syrup at an Indian or Middle Eastern grocer (or search online – UK readers can try www.natco-online.com). The *takmaria* seeds are a wonderful, intriguing touch, although they might be tricky to find – your best bet is an Indian grocer but, if you can't find them, leave them out.

In *Khoja* culture, this drink is celebratory and special: Rose tells me it's traditionally served when an engagement is announced or to celebrate important religious occasions.

For 6 people

1 tablespoon *takmaria* (sweet basil seeds) (optional)
1 litre/1¾ pints semi-skimmed (skim) milk
150ml/5fl oz/¾ cup condensed milk
170g/6oz can evaporated milk
3 tablespoons rose syrup

TO SERVE

6 small scoops vanilla ice cream
25g/1oz/¼ cup shelled pistachios, very finely chopped
40g/1½oz/½ cup blanched almonds, very finely chopped

If you're using the *takmaria*, soak the seeds in 250ml/8fl oz/1 cup of water for 20 minutes.

Blend the milks and the rose syrup together, with a hand-held blender if possible. If you're using *takmaria*, drain the swollen seeds and add them. Cover the *sherbat* and chill well, for at least an hour.

When you're ready to serve, pour the rose-coloured milk into tall glasses, taking care to distribute the *takmaria* seeds evenly (if you've used them). Add a scoop of ice cream to each glass and sprinkle with the chopped nuts.

Mango lassi
Keri ni lassi

When it's mango season (usually from late
April to late June), Rose frequently brings
home a case of her favourite Alphonso mangoes.
These mangoes, from India and Pakistan, are a
beautiful, elongated teardrop shape with pale
yellow, waxy skin and an amazing perfume.
Their flesh is soft, sweet and intensely flavoured
and, for a few days, we gorge ourselves on them.
You're most likely to find them sold by the
case at Indian grocers and Asian supermarkets,
although some regular supermarkets have begun
to sell them. If you see them, buy them – you
won't regret it. If mangoes are out of season,
don't despair – many Indian shops (and some
supermarkets) sell canned mango pulp (you
can even buy canned Alphonso mango pulp, or
the Kesar variety, which is almost as good). It's
a handy standby for serving as a sauce on ice
cream, in Fruit Pudding (page 182) and very
good for making this cooling yoghurt drink.

....

**2 ripe juicy mangoes, or 400g/14oz can mango
pulp (Alphonso or Kesar variety for preference)**
325ml/12fl oz/1$\frac{1}{2}$ cups yoghurt
Sugar to taste

**Makes about 1.2 litres/2 pints, enough for
4 tall glasses**

....

If you're using fresh mangoes, peel and stone
them, chop the flesh and put into the goblet of
a blender. Add 125ml/4fl oz/$\frac{1}{2}$ cup of water and
blend thoroughly until smooth. Then add the
yoghurt, 625ml/22fl oz/2$\frac{1}{2}$ cups of water, and
blend again until thoroughly combined.

If you're using canned mango pulp, empty the
contents of the can into your blender goblet
with the yoghurt and 750ml/1$\frac{1}{4}$ pints/3 cups of
water. Blend well until thoroughly combined.

Taste the mixture and add sugar as you wish –
but remember it shouldn't be too sickly sweet
or it will lose its refreshing quality. If you're
using canned pulp, you won't need to add
much sugar – it's already sweetened.

Cumin-scented lassi
Chaas

The idea of a savoury cooling drink might seem strange to Western palates, but it is very tasty – and surprisingly cooling. It has a roasted, slightly salty tanginess. It's often served at celebrations and is good with any Indian food, but it's great just on its own as a pick-me-up on a hot day.

2 teaspoons cumin seeds
325ml/12fl oz/1$\frac{1}{2}$ cups natural yoghurt
$\frac{1}{2}$ teaspoon salt

Makes about 900ml/1$\frac{1}{2}$ pints, enough for 4

Put the cumin seeds into a dry frying pan (skillet) and roast them over a medium heat for a few minutes, just until they're aromatic. Remove them to a plate to cool, then crush them roughly using a pestle and mortar.

Put the yoghurt, salt and cumin into the goblet of a blender. Add 750ml/1$\frac{1}{4}$ pints/3 cups of water and blend until frothy. Chill and serve.

Passion fruit juice
Matunda no rus

This juice is sublime – forget the over-sweetened store-bought stuff! The addition of a small amount of salt is a masterstroke, magically enhancing the delicious sour-sweet flavour of the fruit. Served well chilled – with ice if you like – this goes well with any spicy snacks.

10 passion fruit
$\frac{1}{4}$ teaspoon salt
2 tablespoons caster (superfine) sugar

Makes about 900ml/1$\frac{1}{2}$ pints, enough for 4

Halve each passion fruit and, using a teaspoon, scoop out the seeds into the goblet of a blender. Add 500ml/18fl oz/2 cups of water and blend until the seeds are pulverised. Sieve the mixture

into a jug (pitcher), pressing the seeds with the back of a spoon to extract as much juice as possible. Scrape what remains in the sieve back into the blender, add 250ml/8fl oz/1 cup more water and blend again. Pour the mixture through the sieve and into the jug with the rest of the juice, scraping and pressing as before. Discard what is left in the sieve this time round.

Add the salt and sugar to the juice in the jug and stir thoroughly to dissolve. Taste and add more salt or sugar as you prefer (take care not to sweeten it too much – the juice is more refreshing if it is slightly sharp). Put in the fridge and chill for a couple of hours before serving.

This will keep in an airtight non-reactive container in the fridge for a couple of days.

Pistachio-almond milk
Khadho

A delicate blend of reduced milk, spices and chopped nuts, this is the stuff of my wife's childhood. She was a poor sleeper and on bad nights she'd go to Rose's bed and shake her mother awake. Bleary-eyed, Rose would take her daughter down to the kitchen, where she quickly prepared a mugful of this soothing drink (she'd keep a stash of chopped nuts in the fridge for this very purpose). Only half-awake herself, Rose would sit at the table, with her head resting heavily on her hand, and watch her daughter drink, then they'd return to bed – and both would be asleep in no time.

1 mug of milk, whole or semi-skimmed (skim)
1 tablespoon condensed milk (optional)
1 teaspoon sugar, or to taste
Large pinch of saffron strands
Pinch of freshly ground nutmeg
Pinch of ground cardamom seeds
1 teaspoon ground almonds
1 teaspoon very finely chopped shelled pistachios

For 1

Put the milk, condensed milk (if you are using it), sugar and saffron into a pan and bring to the boil. Simmer gently until the volume is reduced by a quarter, then add the nutmeg, cardamom and nuts. Stir well and pour into a mug to serve.

Masala tea
Chai

Sweet, scented and milky, *chai* is the perfect, most authentic thing to serve with any of the fried snacks in this chapter – or try it at the end of a meal, when you've no room for a proper dessert but you want a sweet something. You can buy teabags which have a little *masala* in them already, and they're quick and convenient – but I find even the very expensive ones a bit heavy on the spices. This version, made in the traditional way by simmering milk, tea and *masala* together to infuse them and thicken the liquid, comes from Rose's sister Zubeda. For us, she makes the best *chai* of anyone in the family.

Start by roasting and grinding your own blend of spices (this finely balanced *chai masala* is Rose's recipe, incidentally), and fill your kitchen – your whole house, probably – with the wonderful smell of roasting spices.

FOR THE *CHAI MASALA*

....

25g/1oz cassia bark or cinnamon stick, broken into small pieces

40g/1½oz/6 tablespoons cardamoms

1½ teaspoons cloves

1½ teaspoons peppercorns

Half a nutmeg

2 teaspoons ground ginger

TO MAKE 4 MUGS OF *CHAI*

....

1½ mugs of whole milk

1 rounded teaspoon *chai masala* (see method)

3 English Breakfast teabags

4 teaspoons brown sugar or jaggery, and perhaps some more to taste

Makes 4 mugs (and a batch of *chai masala*)

....

First, make the *chai masala*. Preheat the oven to 180°C/350°F/gas mark 4. Scatter the spices on a baking tray (pan), then roast the spices for 10 minutes (I set a timer as I'm likely to forget!).

When 10 minutes is up, remove the tray from the oven and leave the spices to cool completely. Wrap the cinnamon and nutmeg in a clean, dry tea towel and thump with a rolling pin or hammer to smash into small pieces. Add them and any spice 'dust' to the tray of spices and mix well. Grind the spices in small batches in a coffee grinder or spice mill. Sift the resulting powder through a fine-mesh sieve, and put anything that remains in the sieve back through the grinder. Sieve the result and discard anything that remains in the sieve this time round. Mix in the ground ginger and store in an airtight container, in the dark.

To make your tea, put 3 mugs of water into a medium pan. Add the milk, and set over high heat. Bring to the boil, watching carefully that it doesn't boil over, then reduce the heat slightly to keep the milk simmering for 5 minutes. Add 1 rounded teaspoon of the *chai masala*, the teabags and sugar. Simmer for 5 minutes more, stirring now and again. Discard the teabags and taste the tea to see if you want more sugar – *chai* needs to be quite sweet, to balance the flavour of the spices: if the tea isn't sweet enough, it will taste earthy rather than perfumed. Pour the *chai* into mugs and serve.

Sweets

By rights, this chapter should come first in the book, not last: traditionally, most of the dishes included here would be offered at the beginning of a meal or as guests arrive. Some would be served with savoury dishes such as *poori*, *bhajia* or *channa bateta* alongside them as an appetiser. But nowadays Western culture has made its influence felt and, on special occasions, the serving of sweets has migrated more commonly to the end of a meal, as dessert. The rich sweetness of the dishes reflects their status as treats – most of them use cream or evaporated milk, butter and sugar in abundance. They're not intended to be eaten daily – fresh seasonal fruit is the usual end to an everyday Indian family meal at home. Traditionally, the matriarch sits in state at the head of the table and cuts fruit for the family assembled around her, handing out each segment as it is cut, always starting with the children. When fruit is in peak condition, it's as much of a treat as any rich, sticky dessert – but if you've prepared a special Indian meal for friends, what better way to round things off than with an indulgent homemade Indian sweet?

MOST INDIAN SWEETS have a warm, aromatic quality imparted by spices such as saffron, nutmeg and cardamom. When crushing cardamom for sweet dishes, it's crucial that your pestle and mortar has not been previously used for crushing garlic. Garlic's unmistakable scent may linger, tainting your crushed spice – and your sweet dish. It's best to keep one pestle and mortar for crushing garlic, and another for preparing sweets.

Caramel custard
Chassni vari pudding

Just like crème caramel, this is a wobbly set
custard, drenched in caramel – but this Indian
version is flavoured with nutmeg and cardamom
rather than vanilla. Rose always makes a big
pudding and steams it in a special large dish
in a great saucepan on the stove top, deftly
turning out the whole thing onto a big plate.
I've adapted this slightly, to make six more
manageable individual puddings, cooked in
a makeshift bain-marie in the oven (as you
would for classic crème caramel). You'll need
a roasting pan, some foil to cover it, and six
125ml/4fl oz/½ cup-capacity ramekins, mini
pudding bowls or dariole moulds. They should
turn out nicely onto dessert plates, which looks
pretty if you're serving them to guests. The
custards are best made the day before you want
to serve them: leave them in the fridge overnight
and they'll turn out more reliably – and the
flavours will have infused that bit more, too.

FOR THE CARAMEL

4 tablespoons caster (superfine) sugar

FOR THE CUSTARD

4 cardamoms
500ml/18fl oz/2 cups whole milk
100ml/3½fl oz double (heavy) cream
2 eggs
½ tablespoon caster (superfine) sugar
¼ teaspoon freshly grated nutmeg
4 blanched almonds, finely chopped
6 shelled pistachios, finely chopped

Makes 6 puddings

Set out 6 125ml/4fl oz/½ cup-capacity
ovenproof ramekins, mini pudding bowls
or dariole moulds, ready for the caramel.

Put the sugar in a small pan and place over
medium heat. Using a metal spoon, stir the
sugar around constantly. It will begin to clump
together in a rather unpromising-looking rubbly
mess, but keep going – eventually, it will begin
to melt. When it does, reduce the heat slightly,
keep stirring and use the spoon to break down
any lumps. Cook until it is the colour of runny
honey, then remove from the heat.

Tip a little caramel into each of your dishes
(about 2 tablespoons per dish), quickly swirling
it around to cover the base before it sets (see
picture overleaf, bottom left). Be careful not to
splash yourself with hot caramel – because it's
so sticky, it's impossible to remove quickly, so it
can burn you badly. The dishes will heat up
dramatically as you add the caramel, so take
care and, when you're finished, make sure that
you put them down on a heatproof surface.

Preheat the oven to 140°C/275°F/gas mark 1
and put the kettle on to boil.

Lightly crush the cardamom pods, then take out
the seeds and discard the husks. Crush the seeds
finely (make sure that you do this in a mortar
that is not tainted with garlic, or it will taint your
custard). Mix the milk, cream, eggs, sugar,
nutmeg and crushed cardamom seeds together
in a large jug (pitcher). Stir the mixture well.   »

» Stand your pudding dishes in a roasting pan. While you constantly stir the custard (to help distribute the cardamom and nutmeg), pour it into each of the dishes, but stop when they're two-thirds full. As you near the bottom of the custard, you'll find, despite the stirring, lots of spice lurking there. Spoon it out equally into each of the dishes, until the custard is used up.

Pour enough boiling water into the roasting pan to come halfway up the sides of your dishes. Cover the roasting pan tightly with foil, but leave a corner open for steam to escape. Put the roasting pan in the oven and bake for about 2 hours until the custard is set, but still a little wobbly. The tops of the custards will be very lightly tinged with brown at the edges and slightly cracked. Remove the dishes from the roasting pan and leave to cool. If you can, chill these in the fridge once they've cooled completely (overnight chilling is best).

To turn out each custard, run a palette knife (metal spatula) around the edge of the pudding. Now lift up the pudding and knock it sharply on the work surface to loosen it. Put a serving plate upside down on top and, holding both pudding dish and plate, quickly turn the whole thing over. The pudding should slip tremulously from its dish onto the plate – if it shows reluctance, tap the dish with your hand as encouragement. Sprinkle with the chopped nuts to serve.

Rich semolina pudding
Siro

In the Hindu religion, this butter-rich sweet is given as an offering to the gods; in *Khoja* culture, it's blessed and distributed amongst the congregation as part of religious ceremony. At home, it would traditionally be served at the start of a celebratory meal to welcome guests, with *bhajia* or *papar* (poppadums). Like *lapsi* and *shikhan*, it is now more commonly served at the end of a meal, mimicking Western protocol.

225g/8oz/1 cup unsalted butter
225g/8oz/1⅓ cup coarse semolina
12 cardamoms
170g/6oz can evaporated milk
250ml/8fl oz/1 cup whole milk
½ teaspoon saffron strands, crumbled
225g/8oz/1 cup caster (superfine) sugar
10 shelled pistachios, finely chopped
8 blanched almonds, finely chopped

Enough for 8–10 people

Melt the butter in a large pan set over medium heat and add the semolina. Cook for 15 minutes or so, stirring from time to time, until the semolina turns a darker, toffee-like colour. Meanwhile, bash the cardamom pods to break them open. Remove the seeds and crush them finely using a pestle and mortar (be sure it is not tainted with garlic first). Set the resulting powder aside and discard the husks.

Add the evaporated milk, whole milk, saffron, cardamom powder and 500ml/18fl oz/2 cups of water to the semolina.

Continue cooking, stirring frequently, until the mixture becomes thickened, then add the sugar. Cook, stirring continuously, until the butter begins to pool around the sides of the pan. The mixture should be glistening from the butter and dissolved sugar.

To serve, turn the mixture out onto a large warm platter. Spread the *siro* evenly and smooth with the back of the spoon, then use the tip of the spoon to indent the surface with a pattern of arcs, rather like the scales of a fish. Scatter with the chopped nuts and serve warm (but it's lovely cold, too).

Indian rice pudding
Kheer

You can use any rice to make *kheer* but, when we were testing this recipe, it occurred to me that it might work well with Italian risotto rice. So we tried it, and I'm pleased to say Rose and I think this is an improvement on the original. Risotto rice gives this rich, creamy pudding a slightly lighter texture (with the added benefit that it cooks more quickly than the more usual pudding rice). If you want, you can make it with basmati or pudding (short-grain) rice – but, trust me, the Italian rice gives the best results.

60g/2½oz/⅓ cup arborio (risotto) rice
1 litre/1¾ pints whole milk
2½ tablespoons caster (superfine) sugar
100ml/3½fl oz/½ cup double (heavy) cream
6 blanched almonds, finely chopped
8 shelled pistachios, finely chopped
¼ teaspoon freshly grated nutmeg
8 cardamoms
20 saffron strands

Serves 4

Place the arborio rice in a small pan with 500ml/18fl oz/2 cups of cold water and bring to the boil. Reduce the heat and simmer gently until the rice is completely soft – this will take about 40 minutes. Keep an eye on the rice during that time to ensure it doesn't boil

dry – add boiling water as necessary. When the rice is cooked and only a little water remains in the pan, beat with a wooden spoon until the rice becomes creamy.

While the rice is cooking, put the milk in a pan and bring to the boil. Simmer fairly rapidly (but take care not to scorch the milk) until it has reduced to about half of its original volume.

Add the beaten rice to the milk and simmer gently for 15 minutes. Stir frequently to ensure it doesn't stick. Add the sugar, stir well and simmer as gently as you can manage for another 10 minutes. Remove from the heat and add the cream, almonds, pistachios and nutmeg. Lightly bash the cardamom pods to break them open. Remove the seeds and crush them finely using a pestle and mortar (be sure that it isn't tainted with garlic first). Add the powder to the mixture, and discard the husks. Stir well and then turn the *kheer* out into a serving dish.

Scatter the saffron strands over the *kheer* and stir very briefly, to mix them in rather unevenly (Rose says it's prettier when it isn't evenly mixed – and I agree). You can serve this warm, but it's heavenly served chilled – cover the dish with a clean tea towel and leave to cool completely. Remove the towel, cover with clingfilm (plastic wrap) and chill for a couple of hours before you serve.

Fresh fruits with mango sauce
Fruit pudding

You can use any ripe fruit here – but this particular combination works brilliantly so I see no need to tamper with it, providing all the required fruit is available. Fruit pudding is a lovely way to round off a rich meal – it's light, cooling and refreshing (and healthy too).

6 passion fruit, halved
2 small papaya, peeled and seeded
3 bananas, peeled
1 kiwi fruit, peeled
2 plums, stoned
1 mango, peeled and stoned (pitted)
135ml/5fl oz canned mango pulp (about a third of a can), or 1 large mango, peeled, stoned (pitted) and puréed in a food processor

Enough for 6 people

Scoop the seeds from the passion fruit into a large bowl. Chop all the other fruit finely and add to the bowl. Stir in the mango pulp or purée. Cover the bowl and chill in the fridge for a couple of hours before serving.

ROSE TELLS ME that you can enrich the pudding with a little cream or evaporated milk. I think it's perfect just as it is (and the rest of the recipes in this chapter are rich enough!) but, if you like, you can serve with a little chilled pouring (light) cream, ice cream or plain Madeira-type sponge cake.

Grilled buttered plantain
Gonja

Gonja, or plantain, is a large, starchy member of the banana family. You'll find it in Indian, Asian, African and West Indian shops, sold in either its green, unripe state or very ripe, looking like an oversized, overripe banana heavily patched with brown. The latter is used for this simple sweet. If you're barbecuing, it's the ideal dessert – cook over the coals at the end of the meal.

1 very ripe plantain, peeled
Melted butter for brushing

For 1

Preheat an overhead grill (broiler) to its highest setting. Cut the plantain into 1.5cm-/$^1/_2$in-thick slices. Brush a baking tray (pan) with melted butter, lay the slices on the tray and brush them with butter. Cook under the grill, turning once, until brown on both sides. Eat hot.

DON'T ATTEMPT THIS with overripe bananas; they're just not starchy enough.

Sweet saffron-infused yoghurt
Shikhan

I love this creamy, sweet-scented dish – I could eat a whole serving dish by myself. Traditionally eaten with *Poori* (page 116) alongside vegetarian curries, these days it's more commonly served as dessert, on its own or with Fruit Pudding (page 182). In the old days, *shikhan* would be made by putting homemade yoghurt in a cheesecloth and hanging it up to drain overnight to give a thick, creamy consistency – but modern cooks can use rich, thick Greek-style (plain, strained) yoghurt.

Enough for 6 with *poori*, or more if served to accompany fruit

500ml/18fl oz/2 cups Greek-style (plain, strained) yoghurt
2 tablespoons caster (superfine) sugar
15 saffron strands
10 cardamoms
10 shelled pistachios, very finely chopped
6 blanched almonds, very finely chopped

Put the yoghurt, sugar and saffron in a large serving dish. Lightly bash the cardamom pods to break them open. Remove the seeds and discard the husks. Crush the seeds finely using a pestle and mortar (be sure that it isn't tainted with garlic first). Sprinkle the resulting powder over the yoghurt mixture.

Gently fold the yoghurt mixture to lightly combine the ingredients, then cover the bowl with clingfilm (plastic wrap) and chill the *shikhan* until you are ready to serve. Just before serving, scatter with the chopped nuts.

Carrot halva
Ghajer no halwo

Carrots add their distinctive colour and earthy sweetness to this sticky, fudge-like dessert. *Ghajer no halwo* is wonderful served warm with vanilla ice cream – but it's incredibly rich and sweet, so keep portions small!

   Halwo keeps well for about a week or so. Leave it to cool completely before packing into a storage container and placing it in the fridge. To reheat, warm in a pan with a little evaporated milk and cook until it's dry and sticky again.

. . . .

700g/1½lb carrots, coarsely grated

5 cardamoms

500ml/18fl oz/2 cups whole milk

50g/2oz/¼ cup unsalted butter

2½ tablespoons caster (superfine) sugar

4 tablespoons evaporated milk

½ teaspoon freshly grated nutmeg

12 blanched almonds, finely chopped

12 shelled pistachios, finely chopped

Enough for 6 people

. . . .

Put the carrots in a large, wide pan with 325ml/12fl oz/1½ cups of water and cover. Bring to the boil, then reduce the heat to low and simmer for 15 minutes, stirring from time to time. Meanwhile, lightly bash the cardamom pods to break them open. Remove the seeds and discard the husks. Crush the seeds finely using a pestle and mortar (be sure that it isn't tainted with garlic first). Set the resulting powder aside.

After the 15 minutes have passed, remove the lid from the pan and increase the heat to evaporate any liquid in the pan. Stir the mixture frequently to prevent it sticking.

When all the liquid has evaporated, add the milk to the pan and bring to the boil. Cook rapidly to reduce the milk – when it has almost entirely evaporated, add the butter.

Continue cooking until there is almost no liquid left in the pan, then add the sugar. Stir constantly and continue cooking until the pan is dry. Then add the evaporated milk and, again, cook until there is no liquid left in the pan.

When the mixture begins to stiffen and stick together, add the nutmeg and cardamom powder. Continue cooking, still stirring, until the mixture begins to stick to the pan and forms a ball. Rub a small piece between your thumb and forefinger – if it feels gritty, the sugar has not yet dissolved, so continue cooking for a few more minutes. Turn out into a warmed serving dish and scatter with the nuts. Serve warm.

Milk dumplings in cardamom syrup
Gulab jambu

Traditionally, *gulab jambu* would be drenched in syrup scented with rosewater (hence the name – *gulab* means rose). My mother-in-law, Rose, is not keen on the flavour of her floral namesake, however, so she uses headily aromatic cardamom and a hint of saffron instead. You need to make these a day before you eat them, for best results – an overnight steep in the syrup leaves the dumplings gloriously melting and sticky.

Out of respect for the name, I like to serve mine scattered with some fresh rose petals – a whimsical but pretty touch.

2 tablespoons cardamoms

FOR THE SYRUP

225g/8oz/1 cup caster (superfine) sugar
$1/2$ teaspoon saffron strands

FOR THE DUMPLINGS

40g/$1^1/2$oz/$1/4$ cup plain (all-purpose) flour
1 tablespoon melted butter
110g/4oz/1 cup powdered milk
$1/2$ teaspoon baking powder
$1/2$ teaspoon crushed cardamom seeds
5 tablespoons evaporated milk

Groundnut (peanut) oil for deep-frying

**Makes 24 – enough for 8 people, or
more if served with ice cream**

First, prepare the cardamoms. Bash the pods lightly to break them open, then remove the seeds and crush finely using a clean pestle and mortar (be sure that it has no lingering taint of garlic). Set the resulting powder aside.

Next, make the syrup. Place the sugar and saffron strands in a medium-sized pan and add 750ml/$1^1/4$ pints/3 cups of water. Place over medium-high heat and bring to the boil, stirring constantly until the sugar dissolves. Simmer for about 10 minutes, until the mixture is just beginning to get sticky and syrupy – touch the liquid on the spoon to test it. Add 1 teaspoon of the reserved cardamom powder, stir well, then leave the mixture to cool.

To make the dumplings, put the flour and melted butter into a mixing bowl and work together with your fingertips until evenly mixed. Add the milk powder, baking powder and $1/2$ teaspoon of the reserved cardamom powder and mix thoroughly.

Add the evaporated milk and mix with your hands to bring together into a soft dough. Shape the dough into 2cm/$3/4$in balls (about the size of a cherry tomato).

Prepare your wok or *karai* for deep-frying: fill it to no more than a third of its depth with oil, and place over medium-high heat. When the oil is hot (add a fragment of dough to test: it should float immediately, surrounded by bubbles), add   »

» a small batch of dough balls – 6 if your pan is large – and reduce the heat under the pan to low. Turn the balls constantly as they fry, to brown them evenly – they should take about 4 minutes. When they become a dark, rusty brown all over, remove and drain on kitchen paper. Repeat with the rest of the dough balls.

To soak the balls in the syrup, it's best if you can use a wide, shallow bowl that can hold all of the dumplings in a single layer and keep them fairly well covered in syrup. Wait until the syrup is absolutely cold, then add the dumplings. Turn them gently to coat with the syrup and leave to soak overnight. Turn them as and when you can.

Spiced fried biscuits
Thepla

Perfect with a cup of Masala Tea (page 173), *thepla* are simply fried rounds of dough scented with fennel, nutmeg and cardamom. Medium chappati flour (*atta*) is best for this job – made with wholemeal (whole-wheat) flour, the biscuits tend to absorb too much oil. But if you can't find *atta* (see page 20), use a mixture of half-white, half-wholemeal flours, which works well.

450g/1lb medium *atta*, or 225g/8oz/2 cups plain (all-purpose) white flour mixed with 225g/8oz/2 cups wholemeal (whole-wheat) flour
2 tablespoons melted butter
10–12 cardamoms
1 tablespoon fennel seeds, lightly crushed
$\frac{1}{2}$ nutmeg, freshly grated
175g/6oz/1 cup soft dark brown sugar
Groundnut (peanut) oil for deep-frying

Makes 35–40 *thepla*

Put the *atta* or flours in a bowl and sprinkle with the melted butter. Mix thoroughly. Lightly bash the cardamom pods to break them open.

Remove the seeds and discard the husks. Crush the seeds finely using a pestle and mortar (be sure that it isn't tainted with garlic first). Add the resulting powder to the flour in the bowl, with the lightly crushed fennel seeds, nutmeg and sugar. Mix well by hand, then gradually add warm water, just enough to bring the mixture together into a ball.

Roll the dough to about 5mm/$\frac{1}{4}$in thick and cut into rounds with a biscuit (cookie) cutter.

Prepare your wok or *karai* for deep-frying: fill it to no more than a third of its depth with oil and set over medium-high heat. When the oil is hot (add a fragment of dough to test: it should float immediately, surrounded by bubbles), add a small batch of 4–6 dough rounds. Turn them gently in the oil – they should puff up. When evenly golden-brown and crisp, remove them to a plate lined with kitchen paper to drain. Cook the remaining dough in the same way.

Allow to cool, then pack the *thepla* into airtight containers to store. They'll keep for 2–3 weeks.

Toasted cracked wheat pudding
Lapsi

Making *lapsi* will fill your kitchen with the lovely, nutty smell of the toasting wheat – reason enough to make this unusual, delicious, comforting dessert. It's another one of those sweet Indian dishes that's traditionally served at the beginning of a celebratory meal with savoury titbits like *bhajia*, but in modern times it appears at the end of the meal for a more Westernised manner of serving. Normally, it would be coloured brightly with food dye – but we've left this out as it's not necessary. Serve warm in small portions, with ice cream if you like, at the end of a meal that isn't too heavy because this dessert itself is wonderfully rich.

....

75g/3oz/6 tablespoons butter

1cm/$\frac{1}{2}$in cinnamon stick

7 cardamoms

110g/4oz/$\frac{2}{3}$ cup cracked wheat (bulgur)

1 tablespoon sultanas (golden raisins), roughly chopped

3$\frac{1}{2}$ tablespoons sugar

$\frac{1}{4}$ teaspoon freshly grated nutmeg

3 tablespoons evaporated milk

10 blanched almonds, finely chopped

12 shelled pistachios, finely chopped

Serves 4

....

Melt the butter in a large pan over a low heat. Add the cinnamon stick and 3 of the cardamom pods. When the spices are fragrant, add the cracked wheat and stir to coat well with the butter. Cook gently, stirring frequently, until the wheat turns a deeper golden-brown. It's important that the wheat is all nicely browned before you proceed.

Add 750ml/1$\frac{1}{4}$ pints/3 cups of water and the sultanas, cover the pan and bring to the boil. Stirring frequently, simmer the mixture rapidly until it's almost cooked – it should still have a slight chewiness – and then add the sugar. If the mixture is fairly dry, add more water as needed to cook the wheat until it is completely soft.

Meanwhile, lightly bash the 4 remaining cardamom pods to break them open. Remove the seeds and discard the husks. Crush the seeds finely using a pestle and mortar (be sure that it isn't tainted with garlic first).

When the wheat is soft and almost dry, add the cardamom powder, nutmeg and evaporated milk. Stir well to combine, then turn out into a warm serving dish and decorate with the nuts.

Index

Page numbers in **bold** denote illustrations

Glossary

Atta Chappati flour, milled in three grades: brown, medium and white
Bajra Millet, ground to make millet flour, known as *bajra nu loth*
Besan Chickpea flour (also known as gram flour or *channa nu loth*)
Channa Chickpeas. When hulled and split, they become what is known as *channa dal*
Dal or *Daar* A term used either generally to describe all dried peas and beans, or more specifically to denote hulled split dried lentils; also used to describe a soupy dish made using dried beans. *Dal* is the Hindi word; *daar* is Gujarati
Dhana jiru A blend of ground, roasted coriander (*dhana*) and cumin (*jiru*) seeds
Garam masala A blend of ground roasted spices, usually used in meat cookery
Jaggery Indian unrefined sugar, sold in a block – it is grated or chipped off to use
Karai A curved cast-iron cooking pot, usually with two rounded handles, rather like a sturdier version of a Chinese wok
Kasoori methi Dried fenugreek leaves
Khichri A dish of rice and lentils
Masala Literally 'mixture', this can describe a mix of ground spices, or the basic sauce that's used in the preparation of a curry
Masala daba Round stainless-steel tin containing small cups for storing spices
Masoor Whole brown lentils. When husked and split, they become split red lentils and are known as *masoor dal*
Moong Whole green mung beans. When husked and split, they become *moong dal*
Naan White flatbreads leavened with yeast, traditionally cooked in a clay *tandoor* oven
Pawa Flaked rice, found in Indian shops and health food shops
Rotli Chappatis – unleavened wheat flatbreads, the most common Indian bread
Saak Curry
Tava Curved cast-iron griddle
Urad Whole black lentils. When husked and split, they are known as *urad dal* (they are a pale ivory colour)
Vagar A special preparation by which spice seeds and aromatics are tempered in very hot oil. Also known as *tarka* or *tarko*

Acknowledgements

First and foremost, I'd like to thank my mother-in-law, Rose, without whom this book could not exist. I'm honoured that she took the time to teach me her recipes, and thankful for her endless patience during the sometimes baffling process of making a book.

Love and respect are due to my wife, Salima, who dreamt up the concept for this book, took the beautiful pictures, carefully teased and smoothed out my words, and generally reassured me throughout the whole process.

The recipes in this book have a long history and many contributors down the generations, most directly from Rose's mother, Rhemat, who taught her how to cook. Rose and I would like to offer special thanks to all the people whose personal versions of recipes appear in this book: Zubeda (Zuby) Ismail, Anar Dhala, Zubeda Hirani and Mariam Ismail.

Salima, Rose and I would also like to thank several people who, in various ways, contributed to the making of this book: at Pavilion, our heroine Anna Cheifetz, who saw the potential in our concept and finally made it happen, and Emily Preece-Morrison for her support and guidance; Sheila and Sarah Ali and Zubeda Hirani for checking the *Khoja* names for recipes; Ian Garlick and James St John for camera advice; Labour and Wait and Graham & Green; David Gould at Canby; and, last but by no means least, Jacqui Roche for the loan of her beautiful ceramics for photography.

ROSHAN HIRANI (Rose) is the eldest daughter of a large Indian family and, from the age of 11, it was her job to cook for the family. She has more than 50 years of experience and is well known in her community and neighbourhood as an outstanding cook. She is often called upon to provide food for religious and social occasions; her chapatis are legendary.

SIMON DALEY is Roshan's son-in-law, who has worked as a designer and art director specialising in cookery books for more than 10 years. He is an excellent home cook with a keen interest in the traditions and culture of food. His main aim in this book is to continue the centuries-long process of passing down accumulated wisdom from one generation to the next, by recording his mother-in-law's family recipes.